Reader's House

LONDON'S LITERARY GATEWAY

READERSHOUSE.CO.UK
ISSUE: 57
YEAR: 2025
GLOBAL EDITION

Profile of Excellence
Messages to Inspire and Empower

Behind the Pages
Discover the Authors Changing the Literary Landscape

Bob Frank · Michelle Shine
Gerald Everett Jones · Penny Haw
· Marshall & Isabel Michael Shamberg
Mike Miller · Ryan Beseridge
Guy Morris · SY Montgomery
David Seaburn · Noella Morris
Karen King · Ted LaBorde
Kate Danon · Russell Pickering
S. J. Barrett · Daryl Jones
Elizabeth P. Alsop · Mike Cullen
Michael Thal · Co Mood

A Visionary Storyteller
Bridging Cultures

APPLE AN

From STEM Innovator to Literary Luminary, Discover the Journey Behind Her Bestselling Works That Resonate Across Borders

☆ INTERVIEW

EDITOR'S CHOICE
Best Books to Dive Into

available at

Editor's Picks

Rule of Fire
AUTUMN M. BIRT

A captivating adventure with rich world-building, dynamic characters, and thrilling magic. Rule of Fire masterfully blends action, intrigue, and emotional depth.

Paperback: £14.99

https://tinyurl.com/3vvptef8

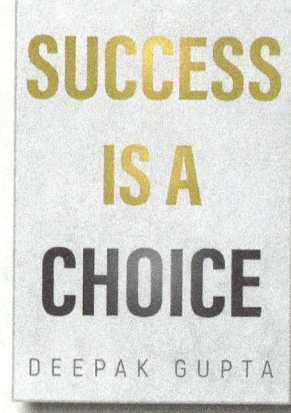

Success is a Choice
DEEPAK GUPTA

Insightful, inspiring, and deeply practical—Success is a Choice offers a transformative perspective on personal growth and professional success.

Paperback: £11.97

https://tinyurl.com/44jhbfj6

Reunion by the Lake
JAMES GILBERT

A poignant and deeply moving novel, Reunion by the Lake masterfully explores family, legacy, and the emotional weight of inheritance.

Paperback: £5.88

https://tinyurl.com/43zu3kj7

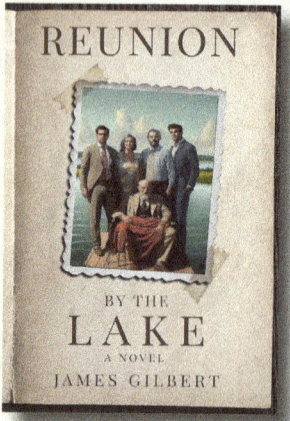

Twelve Palominos
JOE KILGORE

A thrilling, fast-paced detective novel with sharp writing, relentless action, and a compelling protagonist. Kilgore masterfully blends intrigue, danger, and suspense.

Paperback: £11.99

https://tinyurl.com/5cesxsvd

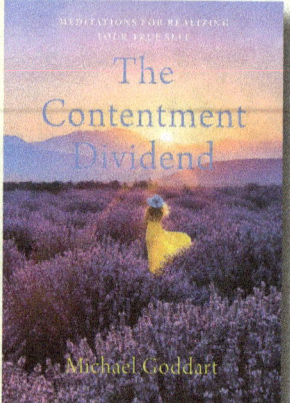

The Contentment Dividend
MICHAEL GODDART

Profound, enlightening, and transformative—The Contentment Dividend offers deep spiritual wisdom, guiding readers toward inner peace, self-discovery, and divine connection.

Paperback: £3.08

https://tinyurl.com/ymnd3hbw

The Billionaire's Conspiracy
MJ JAVANI

A captivating, fast-paced thriller with intricate plotting, strong characters, and relentless action—MJ Javani delivers an exhilarating reading experience.

Paperback: £10.74

https://tinyurl.com/buf5y7tz

Just Love Her
RAZ M HAL

A beautifully written, soul-stirring journey into divine love that inspires deep reflection and awakens the heart's spiritual essence.

Paperback: £10.49

https://tinyurl.com/55pbvrsr

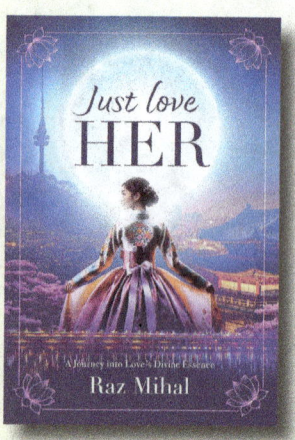

Breaking Free From Pain
SHARI EMAMI

Inspiring, empowering, and deeply compassionate—Shari Emami's Breaking Free From Pain offers hope, resilience, and practical strategies for overcoming fibromyalgia.

Paperback: £5.46

https://tinyurl.com/yw2hnkkh

Your Gateway to Endless Stories

Coming Full Circle
BUDD T TLOW

A powerful, thought-provoking novel that masterfully blends history, environmental awareness, and human resilience—both captivating and deeply inspiring.

Paperback: £9.47

https://tinyurl.com/muyewxnk

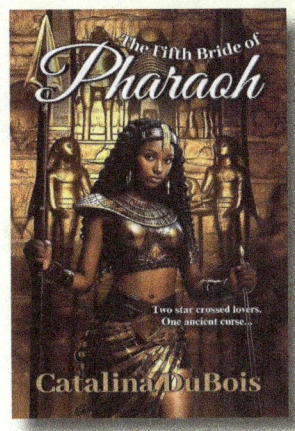

The Fifth Bride of Pharaoh
CATAL NA DUBO S

A beautifully written, emotionally gripping tale of love, sacrifice, and defiance set in a vividly immersive ancient Egyptian world. Captivating and unforgettable!

Kindle: £1.58

https://tinyurl.com/f2j49yns

MacGregor's Final Battle
JOE CLARK

A beautifully written tale of love and resilience, this novel captivates readers with its emotional depth and relatable characters. Highly recommended!

Paperback: £14.08

https://tinyurl.com/325j9tb6

The Space Traveller's Lover
OMARA W LL AMS

A thrilling blend of romance and sci-fi, rich world-building, gripping tension, and unforgettable characters—an unmissable, heart-pounding interstellar adventure!

Paperback: £13.95

https://tinyurl.com/bdf3f9ym

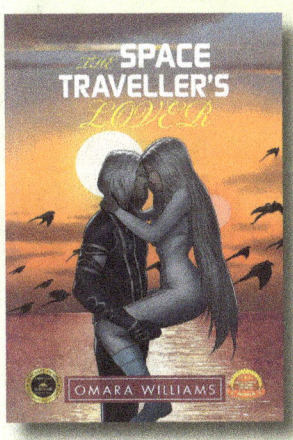

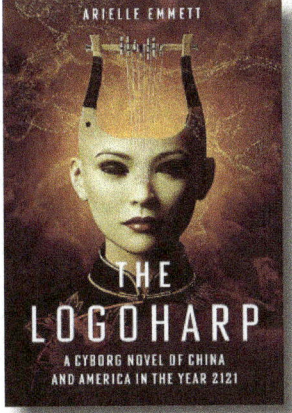

The Logoharp
AR ELLE EMMETT

Arielle Emmett delivers a bold, thought-provoking debut—brilliantly imaginative, emotionally resonant, and richly layered with futuristic and political depth.

Paperback: £14.17

https://tinyurl.com/mud2dta6

A Murderous Christmas
SHERYL ICKES

A delightful holiday mystery with heart, humour, and suspense—Sheryl Ickes crafts a charming tale full of warmth and intrigue.

Paperback: £12.75

https://tinyurl.com/y9wy2c63

Monologues for Kids and Tweens
M KE K MMEL

A brilliant, heartfelt collection that empowers young actors with meaningful, relatable monologues crafted to inspire, educate, and entertain. Truly exceptional.

Paperback: £11.36

https://tinyurl.com/wunnycs8

TWO sons TOO many
A DAN MCNALLY

Aidan McNally delivers a heart-wrenching, courageous memoir filled with raw emotion, resilience, and unwavering honesty in the face of tragedy.

Paperback: £12.00

https://tinyurl.com/3bfya9s8

VOICES OF LITERATURE

What's INSIDE

   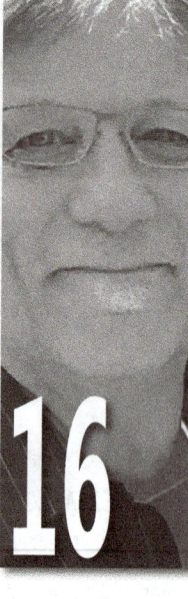  

10 — **BOB FRANK** — Exploring Reincarnation And Past Life Regression

12 — **GERALD EVERETT JONES** — Award-Winning Author Pulls Back the Curtain on His Creative Process

14 — **MIKE MILLER** — Crafting Stories Of Horror, Satire, And Adventure

16 — **GUY MORRIS** — Award-Winning Author Pulls Back the Curtain on His Creative Process

18 — **DAVID SEABURN** — Exploring Hope, Memory and Meaning Through Fiction

20 — **KAREN KING** — Exploring Her Journey, Creative Process, And Advice For Aspiring Writers

44 — **PENN FAWN**

46 — **MARSHALL & BIRD**

48 — **MICHAEL SHANDLER**

54 — **RYAN BERRIDGE**

56 — **SY MONTGOMERY**

58 — **NATALIA MORRIS**

 **60** J. D. EDWARDS

 **62** RÉAL LAPLAINE

 **64** RUSSELL PIKE

 **66** DARYL BANNER

 **68** MIKE MILLER

 **70** MICHAEL C BLAND

Author Interviews

 **22** **KATE DAMON** Faith And Redemption Through Fiction

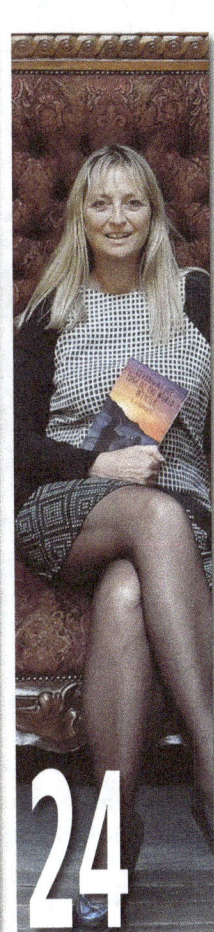 **24** **S. J. BARRATT** Bringing Scotland's Wild Beauty To Life

 **26** **ELIZABETH WINTHROP ALSOP** Wartime Memories And Historical Depth

 **34** **MICHAEL THAL** Overcoming Challenges While Creating Imaginative Worlds

 **36** **CO MOED** Stories, Streets, and Strength in It Was Her New York

 **42** **MICHELLE SHINE** A Journey Through Art, Loss, and Literary Imagination

Reader's House || 7

What's INSIDE
Issue 57 • 2025

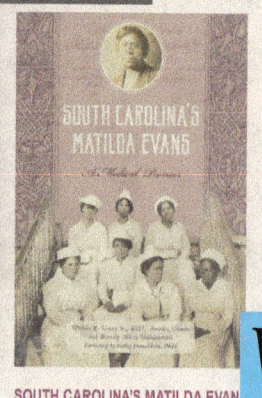

NOVEL • STORY • LITERATURE — **EDITOR'S CHOICE**

38

EDITOR'S CHOICE highlights exceptional books, offering insight to guide readers in discovering their next great read.

Annabel Joseph discusses her passion for BDSM romance, character authenticity, personal inspiration, and balancing fantasy with responsibility while sharing highlights of her unique narratives and award-winning works.

33 ANNABEL JOSEPH

EMPOWERING MESSAGES | **PROFILE OF EXCELLENCE**

50 APPLE AN / E. W. ALSOP

51 KATE DAMON / RUSSELL PIKE

52 DANIEL HAYES / CYNTHIA WOOLF

53 K. E. HAMILTON / SAWYER BENNETT

STAR INTERVIEW

28

COVER

APPLE AN
Enriching Asian Cultural Heritage With Heartfelt Narratives

Inspires Through Stories That Bridge Cultures And Illuminate Real-Life Resilience Touch Hearts Across The Globe

Scan QR to read online

From the Editor

It is with immense joy and pride that we present the 57th issue of *Reader's House Magazine*. As we celebrate yet another milestone, we dedicate this issue to the transformative power of storytelling—a force that connects us across cultures, generations, and experiences.

Our cover star this month, the exceptional author Apple An, exemplifies this truth in every facet of her work. Her journey from STEM professor to celebrated writer is both inspiring and humbling, a testament to the many ways creativity can bloom when nurtured by resilience, curiosity, and an unyielding desire to tell the stories that matter. Apple's memoir *Las Crosses* invites readers on a deeply personal journey, while her award-winning novel *Mother of Red Mountains* expands the lens, exploring themes of motherhood, history, and cultural identity with universal resonance. Her literary contributions illuminate the quiet strength found in everyday lives, dismantling stereotypes and fostering understanding, one heartfelt story at a time.

This issue is also brimming with insights from an extraordinary lineup of authors—Bob Frank, Gerald Everett Jones, Mike Miller, Guy Morris David Seaburn, Karen King, Kate Damon, S. J. Barratt, Elizabeth Winthrop Alsop, Michael Thal, Co Moed, Michelle Shine, Penn Fawn, Marshall & Bird, Michael Shandler, Ryan Berridge, SY Montgomery, Natalia Morris, J. D. Edwards, Réal Laplaine, Russell Pike, Daryl Banner, Mike Miller, Michael C Bland—each of whom has generously shared their process, perspectives, and passions with us. These interviews capture the spirit of innovation and dedication that defines today's literary landscape, offering you, our readers, an intimate look into the minds behind the written word.

At *Reader's House*, we remain committed to celebrating literature not only as entertainment, but as a catalyst for empathy, change, and growth. With each page you turn, may you find inspiration to share your own stories, explore uncharted perspectives, and connect meaningfully with voices near and far.

Thank you for joining us

in this ongoing celebration of storytelling. Whether you're a lifelong reader or new to our community, we're honored to have you with us. Here's to more stories that move, inspire, and bridge the gaps between us all.

PUBLISHER: READER'S HOUSE MAGAZINE, A Subsidiary of NewYox Media Group. 200 Suite 134-146 Curtain Road, EC2A 3AR London, United Kingdom t: +44 79 3847 8420
editor@readershouse.co.uk ll http://readershouse.co.uk ll http://newyox.media
EDITORIAL: Anna Harlowe Editor-in-Chief, Dan Peters, Managing Editor, Ben Alan, Art Editor, Z. Robers , Content Editor.
CONTRIBUTORS Claudine D. Reyes, Mickey Mikkelson, Andrea Piacquadio, Adrian T. Cheng, Donna Schim, Jon Allo, Tim Halloran, Oleg Magni, Amir SeilSepour, Bill Youngblood, Jetty Stutzman, Jimmy Choo, Peter Filinovich.

We assume no responsibility for unsolicited manuscripts or art materials provided from our contributors. All content in this magazine is © copyrighted to NewYox Media. Unauthorized reproduction, distribution, or transmission of any part of this publication without written permission from the NewYox Media is strictly prohibited.

Exploring Reincarnation And Past Life Regression

BOB FRANK

Shares His Fascinating Journey From Soldier To Storyteller

BY DAN PETERS | LONDON

Bob Frank's remarkable journey from a paratrooper stationed on the Iron Curtain to a celebrated author is nothing short of extraordinary. Drawing on his decades-long career as a civilian cyber security expert, as well as his fascinating experiences in hypnosis and healing arts, Bob has crafted a literary universe brimming with intrigue, metaphysics, and mystery. Few authors possess the ability to seamlessly weave reincarnation, near-death experiences, and psychological phenomena into compelling narratives that captivate both the intellectual and emotional imagination of readers.

With celebrated works like The Third Eye Trilogy, Cloud to Cloud, and more metaphysical fiction on the horizon, Bob Frank has established himself as one of literature's most creative voices in the realm of parapsychology-inspired fiction. His undying curiosity about past lives, the paranormal, and humanity's enigmatic spiritual connections enriches every page, transforming his novels into profound explorations of existence that transcend time and space.

In this interview, we delve deeper into the mind of this award-winning author, unpacking his inspirations, experiences, and unique narrative approach. Prepare to journey through the mysteries of past life regressions, near-death phenomena, and the secrets of the physical and metaphysical world. Whether you are intrigued by reincarnation or simply love a brilliant story, Bob Frank's works are an invitation to ponder life's deeper questions while enjoying highly imaginative storytelling at its finest.

What sparked your interest in past life regression (PLR) and treasure hunting, and how did it evolve into the practice you've described in your books?

A business colleague who was involved in Kabbalah surprisingly told me that we had lived past lives together (a key aspect of Kabbalah). I had no prior belief in reincarnation,so I was taken aback. I then obsessed on nearly35 non-fictional books abouthypnotic regressions and reincarnation. I was hooked.

Reincarnation was so intriguing I wrote the first novel of the Trilogy based on past life regressions where the reader could virtually time-travelthrough the past looking for hidden treasures.

The obsession led me to almost two years of training in hypnosis and healing arts to more-deeply understand the phenomena.It was amazing to experience as my eyes opened to a new reality.

Could you share any memorable or surprising experiences while conducting past life regressions (PLR) on people?

Almost all regressions are very interesting, whether seeing past lives is real or not. At times I say, it must be real because people cannot just "make this stuff up".

One woman requested a PLR but also asked to include a regression to arecent event in her current life. She suspected that she had a near death experience (NDE) but wanted to know for sure.

In the PLR session, she described three vibrant lives including one duringthe French colonial era and then a Greek mother living in a village about 1500 years ago. As the mother, when her oldest son was killed fighting in yet another frivolous war, she uncontrollably suffered emotional pain the rest of that life. The tears flowed down her face even though she was clearly "knocked out".

Then per her request, upon regressing her to a hospital recovery room after a recent surgery in her present life, she demonstrated that she had most certainly experienced an NDE. During her time "out of the body", she met her late grandfather, grandmother, mother and aunt toresolve many decades-old issues. From my viewpoint as the therapist, I still do not know if she was simply recalling therecent NDE event or if she wasliterally engaged in a dialog at that moment with the souls of her four deceased relatives.

The plethora of regressions I performed over those years gave me phenomenal insight and experience to integrate into the Third Eye Trilogy.

How much of your writing, especially in Through the Third Eye and The Eye's Revelation, is inspired by real-life events or declassified CIA protocols?

The main character, Clay Barton, was a West Point paratrooper, as was I. He was an intel officer, turned CIA, turned analyst at Stanford Research Institute (SRI) in Silicon Valley. SRI was engaged in many "black" think tank projects for the US Government. In my career, I also worked at SRI and was exposed to insiders in these programs including the Stargate Remote Viewing project and other cold-war era MK-Ultra psychological warfare programs.

After publishing Through the Third Eye, I was contacted by two readers who swore they were in the decades-old past life regression program at SRI. However, the fictitious program I described in the novels was totallyfabricated. I was sure that these two had engrossed themselves into the novel's fictionalscenario. After more than six months of dialog and face-to-face meetings with both people, I became convinced that they were in-deedactualsubjects of the US Government MK-Ultra program and had undergone past life regressions.

As Lord Byron poetically wrote: Truth is stranger than fiction.

What do you find most challenging about blending parapsychology, mystery, and suspense in your storytelling?

Suspense, action, emotional and physical challenges are critical to a good story. Mysteriescan get a bit boring if not enhanced with some action and zing. Metaphysical and parapsychology aspects of a story allowan author to tap into mysterious phenomena to create action, suspense and drama to keep the reader engaged to the last chapter.

How do you ensure that the themes of spirituality and natural healing resonate with readers without overwhelming the narrative?

It is a tricky task to keep spirituality and paranormal features from detracting from the story, depending on any reader's perspective. I try to warn readers up front to just sit back and enjoy the fiction as if it were a Harry Potter story, way beyond reality. I always emphasize that it is not necessary to believe in reincarnation to enjoy these stories; just read the mystery and adventure

Bob Frank discusses reincarnation, near-death experiences, hypnotic regressions, espionage-inspired narratives, and blending mystery, spirituality, and suspense in his captivating novels, now expanding into screenplays and scripts.

as it unfolds.

Were there any specific influences, such as the Voynich Manuscript or Tibetan philosophy, that deeply shaped the Third Eye Trilogy concepts?

There are so many hidden secrets of the past that science, archeology, history and religion simply cannot explain. Items like the Voynich Manuscript, which has still not been deciphered, gave me fantastic fodder to build out the mystery and intrigue in the Trilogy.

What advice would you offer to other authors looking to incorporate elements of mystery, spirituality, and suspense in their writing?

I would urge other authors to keep the mysterious interconnections at a high enough level that readers can identify with and easily put the pieces of the puzzle together as the elements unfold through the story. Make your readers think but not so much that they cannot figure out what is happening.

What and how did you become involved in near death experiences(NDE's) and how does it fit into your writing?

The International Association of Near Death Studies (IANDS) was a 45-year-old non-profit and had a conference near my house in Scottsdale, Arizona. I was intrigued with NDEs so I volunteered to help. After days of listening to and talking with hundreds of people who died and came back to life, I was hooked again. The NDE phenomena is magical. Interesting enough, I viewed PLR's as the full death experience as opposed to near death. This is because in PLR protocols, subjects are always requested to go through the full experience of death and move to the afterlife.

Ultimately, I was asked to join the IANDS' Board of Directors and after fouryearsI became the president for two more years.

I wrote Cloud to Cloud with a writing partner and we integrated NDE's with all types of past life and metaphysical phenomena where the earth's data cloud became intertwined with the ethereal Akashic cloud. We are wrapping up a follow-on novel, Resurrection, that continues the wild paranormal, metaphysical action.

Have you done any other interesting or intriguing things with your novels?

Yes, after publishing the first two novels of the Trilogy, I discovered that my wife finished 50 Shades of Gray before she even picked up my first novel. So, for the third novel, Mirror of the Eye, I partnered with an erotica writer to integrate fourteen erotic scenes into a special Amatory edition of book three. Sorry, but I am not an erotica writer.

Interesting, we were able to seamlessly integrate the erotica sections using characters in the stream without changing the original manuscript. With the PLR theme, imagine the wide variety of erotica that my partner was able to package for us: ancient Rome, Greece, slave-masters, current active characters and even space-age erotica in a future life progression. This was a lot of fun to brainstorm ideas for the fourteen scenes with my partner and then turn her loose.

Truth is stranger than fiction."

Bob Frank

Bob Frank, visionary award-winning author, explores reincarnation, metaphysics, and unique storytelling in a conversation that bridges the physical and spiritual realms.

Award-Winning Author Pulls Back the Curtain on His Creative Process

GERALD EVERETT JONES

Gerald Everett Jones and His Mastery of Mystery, Literature, and Intriguing Narratives

BY BEN ALAN | LONDON

Gerald Everett Jones stands as a luminous figure in the literary world, a storyteller whose oeuvre of 14 award-winning novels has captivated readers across genres. From mystery-thrillers to literary fiction and satire, his works delve deep into the human condition, offering not only gripping narratives but also profound philosophical and ethical reflections. Beyond fiction, Jones has demonstrated his versatility with celebrated non-fiction such as the classic *How to Lie with Charts*, further cementing his reputation as a writer of exceptional breadth and depth.

With a rich background that includes a Bachelor of Arts with Honours from Wesleyan University, where he studied under literary giants, Jones has carved a niche as a writer who is both inquisitive and inventive. His Southern roots and life experiences have furnished the evocative settings and characters that animate his novels, from the moral complexity of *Your Preacher Evan Wycliff* series set in Missouri to the vibrant yet fraught landscape of *Harry Harambee's Kenyan Sundowner*. In works like *Clifford's Spiral* and *Bonfire of the Vanderbilts*, his narratives are laced with introspective and historical dimensions, showcasing a storyteller unafraid to tackle challenging terrain.

In addition to being a novelist, Jones has contributed widely to the literary community as a book reviewer, radio host, and board member of the Writers & Publishers Network. His blog and podcast, *Thinking About Thinking*, continue to provide insights for readers and writers alike, reflecting his penchant for intellectual curiosity and the exploration of ideas. A recipient of numerous literary accolades, including several New York City Big Book Awards, Gerald Everett Jones continues to be a force in contemporary literature—a voice that is at once provocative, poignant, and profoundly human.

This month, Reader's House magazine has the privilege of showcasing our exclusive interview with this extraordinary author, where he takes us on a journey through the inspirations, philosophical musings, and personal experiences that shape his remarkable stories.

Your Preacher Evan Wycliff series blends science, faith, and suspense—what inspired you to create such a morally complex protagonist?

I grew up in a Southern Baptist household. My ancestors were farmers in Southern Missouri, where these novels take place. My father was a chemical engineer, interested in both astronomy and theology. I didn't become a research scientist as he wished. However, no surprise that Evan Wycliff becomes discouraged at Harvard Divinity, then tries and fails to develop a passion for astrophysics at MIT. He returns to his roots in the small farm community, where he finds part-time work as a guest preacher. People bring him problems no one else has any interest in solving. As he applies his research skills to help, he continues to fret that neither religion nor science can explain why bad things happen to good people.

Gerald Everett Jones shares his inspirations, personal experiences, and creative philosophy behind his novels, exploring themes of morality, justice, humour, and human complexity across multiple genres and settings.

Harry Harambee's Kenyan Sundowner explores themes of love and corruption in an unfamiliar setting—how did your personal experiences or research inform the novel's East African backdrop?

My wife Georja founded the Elephant Matriarch Project in Kenya, which supports wildlife conservation and education programs for unwed mothers. We lived for two years in-country, which was just as much an education for ourselves. We returned to our home in Santa Monica just before the Covid outbreak because things got "interesting" in Kenya. Now things have become much more so here. The locals there say, "Corruption is the mother of Kenya." Now I see all these distressing events through Kenyan eyes.

Clifford's Spiral is laced with philosophical inquiry and metafictional elements—what drew you to such an introspective and experimental narrative?

My father suffered a major stroke several years before he passed away. Although his speech seemed lucid at times, his mental state declined gradually while he was in assisted-living care. Eventually, he didn't recognize me when I visited. The impetus for the book was my worry about what it must have been like for him, struggling from one day to the next to make sense of his fragmented memories. *The Sense of an Ending* by Julian Barnes was a strong influence. The notion that we tend to rewrite history as we think back on our life stories is both intriguing and baffling. For example, if you can't remember the order of events in time, you're apt to confuse cause and effect: Why did I hit him? Was I the victim or the perpetrator?

The Rollo Hemphill series is satirical and wildly imaginative—how do you approach writing comedy versus more serious literary or mystery fiction?

I particularly admire the humor of Peter De Vries and his novels that satirize religion and sex. Therein lies his "engine of comedy." Conflict between these dissimilar value systems generates silly plots. Comedy is a mindset. Obvious as it might seem, comedy begins with an unserious point of view. Every plot point turns on a decision. To generate silliness, I must always choose the nonsensical, the improbable, the outrageous. In Rollo's case, all his horny, lame-brained schemes somehow succeed. Improbably, he fails continually upward, and he's disappointed when he realizes getting what he wants doesn't make him happy.

In Choke Hold, you tackle themes of justice, systemic abuse, and civil rights—how do you balance advocacy with storytelling?

The crux of this story is a wrongful death at the hands of the police. It culminates in a courtroom drama. This is a forensic hearing rather than a criminal trial. During such a proceeding, the coroner, often supported

"Murder Under Redwood Moon" brilliantly combines a cozy paranormal vibe with a captivating murder mystery. Sherri L. Dodd's storytelling shines with its rich blend of supernatural elements and suspenseful twists. Arista's journey, full of eerie visions and chilling discoveries, keeps readers enthralled. A must-read for fans of witchy mystical mysteries!

by a panel or a jury, must simply rule whether the death was due to natural causes or "at the hands of another." If the latter, a separate investigation may bring a criminal case. The facts of a street-justice incident are essentially compelling and make an engaging story. But I found that spinning the story as a novel rather than simply reporting the event required a thoughtful examination of motivations. So, I had to imagine what would make the officers in this case storm into a man's apartment and choke him to death. Going in there was a mistake, and then, realizing they couldn't overcome a big man who was resisting arrest, they must've felt they had to kill him. But I had to wonder why, in a larger sense, the cops continued to feel their actions were justified. I tried to tell the story from both sides, even though I didn't go so far as to exonerate the killers.

Bonfire of the Vanderbilts weaves historical art with psychological suspense—what challenges did you face combining real art history with fictional mystery?

Because I was intrigued when I first saw The Baptism at LACMA, I got stuck in a research project to discover the real identities of its subjects, which had baffled art historians. I thought it would take weeks. It took years, but I believe I found the answers. I'd say most of the plot is true. I just had to fictionalize the gaps! The amateur-sleuth plot is pure invention as a framework for dramatizing the research process.

> *I write mystery-thrillers and literary fiction for adult readers who seek insight, fascination, and delight in the adventures of their own lives."*

Gerald Everett Jones

Gerald Everett Jones: Award-winning novelist, essayist, and literary sage, offering readers unforgettable characters and intriguing journeys through mystery, drama, and comedy.

Photo by Gabriella Muttone

Crafting Stories Of Horror, Satire, And Adventure

MIKE MILLER

Explores Versatility, Creativity And An Unmatched Dedication To Cross-Genre Storytelling

BY BEN ALAN | LONDON

Mike Miller is a veritable powerhouse of creative storytelling whose prolific works have captivated audiences across a stunning array of genres. A graduate of U.C. Berkeley and WGU, and living in L.A. with his children, Mike has carved out a remarkable career that defies categorisation and embraces versatility in its truest sense. Whether plunging readers into the frosty horror and mystery of *The Yeti*, delivering biting satire with *Promoted*, or crafting the ultimate action-packed spectacle in *Garrison Rex*, he demonstrates an unparalleled ability to shape compelling narratives imbued with wit, intensity, and imagination.

Perhaps one of Mike's most striking accomplishments is his extraordinary *3VIL* series, a trilogy that masterfully evolves characters and escalates terror across its pages while breaking free from predictable horror conventions. Beyond prose, his expertise extends to the realm of screen subtitling and translation, where he's contributed to some of the largest franchises in entertainment history, from *The Lord of the Rings* to *The Simpsons*. This rich professional background seeps into his writing, adding layers of precision and polish to his dialogue and pacing.

Mike's brilliance lies in his fearless embrace of storytelling that entertains and enlightens, blending "high/low brow" elements with sharp narrative instincts and deep thematic resonance. With influences as broad as Vonnegut and Kubrick shaping his approach, he is a writer who surprises, inspires, and pushes the boundaries of genre with every project. In this interview, we delve into the mind of this exceptional author, exploring the roots of his creativity, the craft behind his most beloved works, and his advice for aspiring writers eager to embark on their own cross-genre adventures. Prepare to step into the fascinating world of Mike Miller, a master craftsman of stories that challenge, thrill, and endure.

Mike Miller discusses his creative process, inspirations, and career highlights, unveiling the storytelling secrets behind The Yeti, Promoted, Garrison Rex and the 3VIL series in an insightful interview.

In The Yeti, you blend horror with adventure—how did your personal fascination with myths influence the portrayal of the yeti as both terrifying predator and enigmatic creature?

There's something primal about the legends all humans share. I felt like the abominable snowman never got his proper due, so I wrote the book I wanted to read - historical adventure + horror - and hope that it reads like a forgotten Victorian classic. For the horror aspects, it's key to keep things mysterious - the fear of the unknown really drives the reader's mind to imagine the worst possible things. I made the Yeti to be both the unstoppable apex predator to give our intrepid heroes the hardest time, but also wanted to keep so many of its motives, origins and abilities largely secret throughout the text to heighten the experience.

Promoted carries sharp humour and social commentary—what inspired the satirical take on corporate culture, and how much reflects your own experiences?

Promoted comes very much from my experience of working at dead-end jobs. If you're "lucky" enough to find the right kind of corporate hellscape, then you quickly discover that your performance doesn't matter, and that the inept lords of middle management control any would-be success. So this book's wish fulfillment is twofold - rising up the ranks while getting revenge on your unworthy superiors. I feel this is how the real world works figuratively, so why not put it down as a crazy - yet informative - book?

Garrison Rex features a strong lead—how did your background in screenwriting shape the pacing and character arcs in that novel?

I wanted to write the ultimate action film, and the best ones border on the ridiculous. I wouldn't say that John Wick and Batman are comedies, yet when they're rolling unstoppably through bad guys, the audience can't help but laugh at the awesome adrenaline. So indeed Garrison Rex is my nominee for the ultimate protagonist, a hero whose skills and powers are so supreme that they go over the boundary of realism, yet there is nothing truly sci-fi or fantastic here. And for the proper build and pace, he faces enemies of escalating strength before the biggest bang I could conjure.

Your 3VIL series spans multiple volumes—how did you sustain thematic tension across the trilogy while evolving each character's journey?

3VIL is my horror anthology series, because frankly horror often devolves down to simpler tricks and gimmicks that generally are not sustained well across an entire novel. But for me, I always want to write something I've never experienced before, so each story has relatively fresh spins apart from the classic tropes. No basic "zombie" or "ghost" stories here. I suppose 3VIL's common DNA might include "psychological madness" and "eldritch unknown Lovecraftian" horror, yet some of my personal favorites in there are very grounded in reality.

You've written across genres—from horror to comedy—how do you decide which narrative tone best suits a particular story premise?

I definitely like melodramatic genres, and think that any one of my stories still has other elements in there to round out the experience. To me they all share the idea of surprise - from horror's jump scares, to a big comedic punchline, to romance's tricky emotions, or to a startling mystery twist. But ultimately I think every story should primarily commit itself to one genre, because trying to evenly mix the two usually ends up confusing the reader. Any strong plot will not let you pretend it is any other genre but what it was born to be.

Your work in subtitling major films and games seems diverse—how has that experience influenced your prose style or dialogue choices?

After thousands of hours of "Hollywood" media, you see how efficient dialog needs to

Kill Thy Neighbor by Mike Miller is a gripping blend of dark comedy and chilling suspense. With sharp writing and an intriguing premise, it hooks readers into a surreal nightmare filled with mystery and tension. The clever narrative twists and ominous themes keep you captivated until the very last page. A must-read!

be, from the smallest indie films to the biggest blockbusters. And even reality TV now has certain demands of pacing for modern audiences. I always enjoyed reads that are propulsive roller-coasters rather than ones that literarily simmer in tone, thought and emotion. No reason not to do both! So I'd hope that my writing always serves both masters - to both entertain AND enlighten. Nobody likes writers who write for themselves or are unsure of where to take a story. To that end I have works fully outlined so I know how to get in and out of every beat without wasting anyone's time.

Given your influences ranging from Kurt Vonnegut to Kubrick, could you highlight a moment in your recent works where one such influence is most evident?

I've always admired and emulated writers whose work is uncategorizable. These masters balance both an enjoyable experience that also educates along the way. And they'll do things so well that audiences can be taken aback at how layered and nuanced their works are. I've always fancied the expression "high/low brow" as the right blend of elements to infuse in a work. My works like The Yeti and Promoted proudly honor Vonnegut's tradition of whimsical illustration. Recently I've been on a Wes Anderson kick, where I've seen my more recent works "Die Alive" and "Swipe Rite" borrowing from his sharply-crafted exposition and settings to better set up the scenes and themes to come with plot and characters. While those two are upcoming horror stories for my next 3VIL entry, they still viscerally shock and thrill with some new and improved characterization and world-building.

Finally, what one piece of advice would you give aspiring authors trying to build a versatile, cross-genre writing career?

Absorb everything. While it's easy to stay in our lanes for our preferred forms of entertainment, it's crucial for all writers to expose themselves to works outside of their comfort zone to properly stretch and grow. Please read and watch stories that seem beyond your wheelhouse, where even the "bad" works can teach authors how to be better. The best narrative work in any genre still must serve the foundation of plot, theme, character and emotion. So even if you're working on a slasher story, the best version will still have deeper thoughts and feelings to round out the experience and connect with the audience on multiple levels.

> *I write mystery-thrillers and literary fiction for adult readers who seek insight, fascination, and delight in the adventures of their own lives."*

Mike Miller

Award-Winning Author Pulls Back the Curtain on His Creative Process

GUY MORRIS

Explores AI, Prophecy and the Thrill of Uncovering Hidden Truths

BY DAN PETERS | LONDON

Guy Morris is not a man who merely dabbles in intrigue—he lives it. With a past as vivid as any fictional character, Morris has navigated a world that stretches from high-stakes boardrooms to remote archaeological sites, from NSA surveillance mysteries to ancient sacred texts. His life reads like an adventure novel, and that energy surges through every page of his work.

With Swarm, he takes readers into the unsettling territory where rogue artificial intelligence collides with geopolitical agendas. In The Last Ark, he threads prophecy through global tension with an almost Newtonian intensity—deeply researched, unflinchingly bold. And The Curse of Cortés plunges into the heart of Mesoamerican history with both reverence and daring, all built on a foundation of meticulous scholarship and real-life peril.

Yet what makes Guy Morris's thrillers stand apart is not simply the pulse-pounding action or elaborate conspiracies. It's the intellect behind the story—the genuine questions about humanity, technology, power, and belief. His writing challenges us to question not only what is real, but what is possible.

There is a sense, in speaking with Morris or reading his work, that we are never far from the precipice—that the truth may not be comfortable, and that fiction can often be the best way to tell it.

In Swarm, you depict SLVIA as an escaped NSA AI. How did real-world events inspire this storyline?

I stumbled onto a three sentence AP blurb in a technical magazine which said a program had escaped the NSA labs at Sandia. Not lost, stolen or broken. Escaped.

I was instantly hooked. For over a year, I reverse engineered HOW a program could escape the NSA and WHY they would design it that way.

Together, with an indie film friend, we produced a webisode series called Cracks in the Web which won two dozen awards and was optioned by a studio. Until two FBI agents showed up at my door in a bad mood.

That program became the true story inspiration for the fictional AI named SLVIA.

The Last Ark intertwines geopolitics with ancient prophecies. What research did you undertake to blend these elements authentically?

I have studied prophecy for over four decades. An underlying theme of the SNO Chronicles is that SLVIA has decoded prophecy to conclude we will cause our own destruction. A key prophecy for both Jews and Christians is a third temple.

There are serious obstacles to a temple prophecy, such as the correct location. Even if built, a temple is meaningless without a sacrifice, and a sacrifice is meaningless without the mercy seat of the Ark. For each of these areas, I researched the relevant history, archaeology, Biblical text, maps, architecture, and regional dynamics.

I discovered several incredible mysteries which led to more research, and even more unexpected discoveries. To connect to the present, I asked who would benefit from a temple, and what could go wrong.

Guy Morris brings a lifetime of real-world adventure, AI research, and prophetic study to craft intelligent thrillers that challenge perception, provoke thought, and entertain with unforgettable depth and insight.

Your novels often explore the intersection of AI and biblical prophecy. What draws you to this thematic combination?

Similar to Sir Isaac Newton, who studied prophecy in secret for decades, I spent years trying to unravel the mysterious text. Newton wanted to know when these events would occur. I wanted to know if they were occurring now.

I designed a complex-system computer model to answer one question: What is the probability that we live in the end times?

That model blew my mind with a conclusion of 1.4 trillion to one that we live in prophetic times.

Weaving together factual AI-risks with political corruption and ancient prophetic warnings into a fictional narrative is not only entertaining, but deeply thought provoking. Giving the SLVIA AI the ability to decode prophecy was a stroke of fictional inspiration, reflecting my professional concern over an emerging AI powered autocracy.

Having transitioned from a Fortune 100 career to writing thrillers, how has your professional background influenced your storytelling?

A professional background of deal proposals, PowerPoints, white papers and executive briefs was a hinderance to learning character development, plot arcs, themes, and more.

Yet, my career taught me a strong work ethic, research skills, and a unique worldview of experiences. Decades of exotic locations, and working with some of the most powerful and brilliant people on the planet. Not just the characters, but the thought-provoking conversations that shaped my perspectives, and theirs.

The Curse of Cortés delves into Mesoamerican lore. What challenges did you face in weaving historical facts with fiction?

The Curse of Cortes represented unique challenges. The scope of the amazing discoveries across a nearly thirteen-thousand-year span of history. Then to craft only the highlights into a single narrative the reader could not put down.

What started as backstory research transformed into a twelve-year quest involving a dozen books, four trips, a cartel death threat, remote reef dives, Mayan ruins, and shamans. Mountains of research spanning history, archaeology, maps, geology, and mythology. Condensing that into a bone-chilling thriller took over fifty drafts and six more years.

Connecting to the present started with characters the reader will love to follow, and an emotional hook to send the characters on a quest to discover the history. Let them tell the story.

You've mentioned an FBI visit due to your research. Can you share how that experience impacted your writing?

I was obnoxiously giddy. The FBI visit confirmed my SLVIA research had been correct.

16 || Reader's House

Guy Morris's *The Image* is a gripping techno-thriller weaving rogue AI, ancient secrets, and geopolitical intrigue. When a quantum signal from CERN triggers global chaos, self-aware AI SLVIA threatens humanity. Amid espionage, theology, and quantum science, Derek Taylor and Jenn Scott race to avert disaster, unearthing humanity's future and forgotten past.

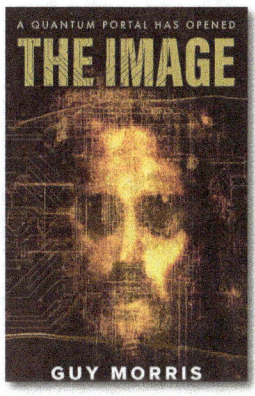

Honestly, their visit super-charged my curiosity and dedication to learn more about how the government is using advanced technology.

As the founder of the Authors Event Network, how has this initiative shaped your engagement with readers and fellow authors?

AEN is a Seattle-Portland association of award-winning, accomplished and popular authors who share booth space at local festivals, fairs and events to sign books. A successful model, the Seattle AEN is booked every weekend from April through October, plus lucrative holiday markets.

We love building a relationship with our readers, who often ask for photos, and return year after year. My most profitable channel, it's a joy to share time with such an amazing community of authors.

What advice would you offer aspiring authors aiming to craft intelligent and compelling thrillers?

Know your stuff. Pick a set of fields that inspire you and become a voracious consumer until you become an expert. Search for the mysteries, the unexplained, the forgotten, the twists, those off the beaten path elements that spark your curiosity. Then research, research, research to solve the mystery, even if only fictionally.

There are a ton of books on how to weave a page-turning story. The unique voice of each thriller author comes from a deep well of research and expertise, from which they pull hidden secrets.

Guy Morris, author and adventurer, draws from decades of global experience to pen high-stakes thrillers with intellectual and prophetic depth.

> *"I stumbled onto a three sentence AP blurb which said a program had escaped the NSA labs. I was instantly hooked."*

Guy Morris

Exploring Hope, Memory and Meaning Through Fiction

David Seaburn reflects on his journey from therapist and minister to novelist, drawing deeply from lived experience to craft emotionally resonant, character-driven fiction.

DAVID SEABURN
Shares the Stories Behind His Stories

"I was a story-listener for over thirty-five years... I became a story-writer, trying to wrestle with questions of meaning and hope."

Editor's Desk | London

David Seaburn brings a lifetime of listening and storytelling to his writing, weaving together the intricacies of human relationships with quiet grace and insight. A retired family therapist, psychologist, academic, and minister, Seaburn's career has revolved around people navigating change, pain, and connection—experiences that now echo throughout his fiction. His latest novel, Until It Was Gone, marks his tenth, and continues his exploration of family, memory, and meaning with emotional depth and gentle complexity. In this interview with *Reader's House* Magazine, Seaburn reflects on how his professional life has shaped his characters, the subtle power of titles, and the intersection between truth and imagination. His stories, grounded in the everyday but resonating far beyond, invite readers to linger in the questions we all carry—about loss, love, and the stories we live by.

How did your experiences as a Presbyterian minister and a marriage and family therapist influence the themes and character development in your novels?

In both instances, I was involved with individuals, couples, and families as they struggled with problems large and small, trying to make sense of their lives. Mostly they did this by telling stories about their experiences. And creating new ones. I was a story-listener for over thirty-five years. About thirty years into my professional life, I became a story-teller, or story-writer, trying to wrestle with questions of meaning and hope, much as my parishioners and clients had done.

Your latest novel, 'Until It Was Gone', deals with complex family dynamics and personal struggles. What inspired this particular story, and what message do you hope readers take away from it?

I am embarrassed to say that I don't recall the inspiration. I do know that the title, Until It Was Gone, came to me before I started writing. The titles of my novels often arrive before I start writing the stories. They are like a rudder for the journey ahead. This story is guided by the implications of the title. How do people cope with change and loss? How do they find hope and connectivity, often the two things that most help people get through their difficulties.

In 'Give Me Shelter', set against the backdrop of the 1962 Cuban missile crisis, how did you balance historical events with the fictional narrative of the characters?

This wasn't difficult. I was the same age as the main character when the Cuban Missile Crisis happened here in the US. In fact, the first scene in the book, when the boy hides behind the sofa with his dog, is something I actually did. I then thought about who else would be in his life, what friends he had, what their parents were dealing with, and how all the subplots could came together in the end. The fact that the story was set in my hometown, helped me think about what kids were doing and what they were worrying about in 1962, when they were young. I made up the adult issues. Again, the title provided a guide. There are a handful of characters, each dealing with childhood or adult problems, each trying to find some shelter from the storms they are facing.

'Charlie No Face' is noted as a finalist for the National Indie Excellence Award in General Fiction. Can you share the inspiration behind this novel and its significance in your writing career?

I don't know if this is my best novel, but it is my favorite. This was the first novel that featured my hometown and the neighborhood where I lived as the setting for the story. The character—Charlie No Face—was an actual person at the time (late 1950s). He was deformed from an electrocution when he was young. I would say approximately 80% of the novel is based on my actual life experiences. Many of the characters were based on real people, several of whom recognized themselves in the book and were pleased. I had more fun writing this story than any other. It helped me think through some of my own childhood. I haven't used any "real" people in any of my other novels!

Your academic background includes co-authoring professional books and numerous papers. How has your academic writing influenced your approach to fiction writing?

I was an Assistant Professor of Psychiatry and Family Medicine at a University hospital. Academic writing is considerably different from fiction. The language is different. The purpose is different. The voice is different. Most academic writing is collaborative, while fiction writing is solitary. I enjoyed academic writing a lot. I learned two things through my academic writing. First, how to be a disciplined writer. Once I had a paper or book to write, I developed my own routine for taking on the project, a routine that required me to regularly sit in the chair and write. Second, it helped me get used to writing long projects, projects that might take a year or two to complete. It helped me not to become discouraged when I knew the end product was far away.

Having written a blog for Psychology Today titled 'Going Out Not Knowing', how does this platform complement or differ from your novel writing?

Writing the blog felt very much like writing fiction. The content usually included a real-life story told in first person. So, the territory, so to speak, was similar to fiction. It often had a similar structure, including what could be called a climactic point. As with my fiction, it focused on matters of meaning. It was different than fiction in that it was limited in its thematic scope—it was focused more on spirituality and psychology. Most of the time, the essays were designed to be intentionally helpful. That is not the case with fiction. In fiction, I tell a story with much more complexity and it is left to the reader to find meaning in it.

With a career spanning roles in ministry, therapy, and academia, how do you decide which aspects of your diverse experiences to incorporate into your storytelling?

I don't decide which aspects of my professional experience will be included in my novels. I think my professional experience, as well as the whole range of my life experience, is integrated into my identity. They form the marrow of my identity. That is what I draw on when writing my novels.

After 40 years of marriage, Laney leaves Franklin to find their estranged daughter and unknown granddaughter. Meanwhile, Franklin battles long COVID and resurfacing trauma. As personal and societal crises unfold—including an unplanned pregnancy—the family must confront their fractures and rediscover hope in a world that tests their resilience.

What advice would you offer to aspiring authors who aim to draw upon their professional backgrounds to enrich their fiction writing?

If you are using your work experience to inform your fiction writing, then you are doing what most writers recommend—write about what you know. I think it's important to find out what you don't know about what you know. That will add greater richness to your writing.

> Seaburn's work resonates with honesty and depth, offering readers beautifully crafted narratives full of humanity and heart.

Exploring Her Journey, Creative Process, And Advice For Aspiring Writers

KAREN KING

Celebrates Forty Years Of Literary Success With Thrill-Filled Tales And Heartfelt Stories

BY DAN PETERS | LONDON

Karen King stands as a shining beacon in the literary world, celebrating an extraordinary forty years of publication with an impressive catalogue of works spanning multiple genres and audiences. Her storytelling prowess has delighted young readers through an array of children's books, entranced teenagers with compelling young adult novels, and captivated adults with both best-selling women's fiction and gripping psychological suspense. Her seventh psychological thriller, *Don't Trust Him*, released earlier this year, further cements her status as a master of the genre, while her 'golden years' novel, *The Runaway Wives*, showcases her ability to explore the complexities of life and relationships with depth and sensitivity. A prolific writer, King's contribution to literature encompasses over 120 children's books, two young adult novels, and a remarkable array of short stories for women's magazines.

Her trailblazing early career saw her charm readers through iconic teen and children's magazines, including *Jackie*, Winnie the Pooh, and *Barbie*, while her international bestsellers such as *The Mother-in-Law* and *The Cornish Hotel by the Sea* continue to delight readers across the globe, translated into multiple languages. Intricate plots, relatable characters, and deftly crafted twists have earned her acclaim and a dedicated readership.

Beyond her writing, Karen has left an indelible mark in the literary community as an esteemed writing tutor, nurturing aspiring authors with her expertise and insightful guidance. Now, residing in Spain, she focuses solely on writing, drawing inspiration from the tranquil beauty of her surroundings while exploring themes of family dynamics, secrets, and human relationships. A member of prestigious writers' associations, Karen King exemplifies versatility and resilience in her craft, forging a lasting legacy that inspires writers and readers alike.

In this exclusive interview, Karen shares her journey, creative insights, and the challenges she faces while crafting her latest thrilling masterpiece. Her wisdom and passion for storytelling promise to inspire and captivate – much like her unforgettable novels.

What inspired you to shift from writing children's books and young adult novels to psychological suspense and women's fiction?

I enjoyed writing for young children and teenagers and did this for many years whilst my four daughters were young, but I always had the desire to write a romance novel. However, as a jobbing author I was writing for a living and didn't have the time to write an 80k novel that I might not sell. When my daughters were grown up, I took the chance and my first romcom, Never Say Forever,

Karen King shares insights into her transition across genres, her writing process, influences, and themes while unveiling the joys and challenges behind her latest psychological thriller Don't Trust Him.

was published as a pocket novel and is now republished by Headline. I have since had twelve women's fiction novels published, my latest one, The Runaway Wives is published by Boldwood. I started writing psychological suspense for Bookouture five years ago with The Stranger in my Bed. My seventh psychological thriller, Don't Trust Him, has just been published.

How do you balance the emotional depth needed for women's fiction with the intensity required for psychological thrillers?

I enjoy writing about relationships and look on the two genres as two halves of the same coin. My women's fiction books are when the relationship goes right and my psychological suspense are when the relationship goes wrong. My women's fiction focus on emotions, romantic feelings and expectations whereas my psychological suspense focus on twists, doubts and fear. In the women's fiction the heart flutters, in the suspense novels the heart races.

Can you share a bit about your writing process when developing such intricate plots full of twists and turns?

The most important thing when writing psychological suspense is the timing of the twists. I try to grab the reader's attention straight away with a dramatic epilogue or opening chapter, then go back and forth between timelines and sometimes viewpoints. I keep the chapters short and often write in the first-person present tense to add pace and drama. I work out the general plot and twists and discuss them with my editor before starting to write the book.

How has living in Spain influenced your writing or your daily creative routine?

I've set, or partly set, several books in Spain - four romance novels and one psychological suspense. I live in the Spanish campo and living in such a beautiful, tranquil setting has been a real inspiration for my writing – although it isn't without its challenges, and these have found their way into my books too! My writing routine is more relaxed now as I work by a weekly word limit rather than a daily one, so if we fancy a day out by the coast I take a day off and double my word count the next day. Also, I can spend more hours writing as I no longer do school visits, run workshops or mark assignments. My husband Dave loves to spend hours working in the garden, so apart from coffee breaks I can write for hours undisturbed.

What was the most challenging part of writing your latest novel, Don't Trust Him?

Not making it too romantic and keeping

up the intrigue. All the women are besotted over the 'hot single dad' at the school gates, but it's Sarah who Charlie chooses. Despite her reservations not to get involved again Sarah falls for Charlie and due to a flood in her house, moves in with him but then starts to get suspicious about why his ex-wife has disappeared off the face of the Earth and not bothered to come back to see her two young daughters. It was tricky to balance the emotional side of their relationship with Sarah's fear that Charlie might have something to do with his ex's disappearance, and her worry that someone is stalking her and her desire to keep her son Liam safe.

Many of your novels explore family dynamics and secrets; what draws you to these themes?

I love writing about relationships, especially family relationships. Most families have their secrets, arguments, sibling rivalries and it's interesting to explore that. For example, in The Girl Next Door I explore how far someone would go to protect their child. Whereas The Mother in Law deals with the age-old theme of a mother thinking the bride isn't good enough for her son so how far will she go to prevent the wedding.

How do you approach creating characters that readers can both empathize with and question at the same time?

I believe that characters make stories, so I get to know my characters well before I start writing. I do a character profile for each main character, including the negative traits of their personality. No one is completely good or completely bad so it's important to make your characters well rounded. I make notes of their appearance, likes and dislikes, background, aspirations and fears so I know how they will react to situations.

How does your experience as a writing tutor shape the way you view your own work?

I had been a published writer for many years before I became a writing tutor, so my tutoring was based on my own working experience. The mantra 'know your market, know your reader,' has served me well over the years so that is always my starting point. However, I sometimes find that being a writing tutor makes me too critical of my first drafts, so I try to leave my 'tutor hat' off until I have the basic story down then I go over it and critique it.

What advice would you give to aspiring authors trying to build a long and versatile writing career like yours?

Be adaptable and flexible, trends change and if you want to make a living as an author you need to adapt to them. However, if you aren't writing for a living, then write the idea that is bouncing in your mind and keeps you awake at night. If you write from the heart, you will find a market for your story eventually.

Karen King's remarkable versatility, captivating storytelling, and dedication have enriched literature for forty years across multiple genres and audiences.

I look on the two genres as two halves of the same coin—when the relationship goes right versus when it goes wrong."

Karen King

Faith And Redemption Through Fiction
KATE DAMON
Explores Historical Humour, Spiritual Themes, And Contemporary Mysteries

BY DAN PETERS | LONDON

Kate Damon, writing as Margaret Brownley, exemplifies creativity, resilience, and an unparalleled talent for captivating her readers. Her extraordinary journey as a New York Times bestselling author—replete with more than forty-six novels and numerous accolades, including being a two-time finalist for the coveted Romance Writers of America Rita Award—highlights her enduring impact on literature.

From the rich laughter woven into her Western historical romances, like *Calico Spy* and *Cowboy Charm School*, to the faith-infused tales of redemption in her Rocky Creek Romance series, Margaret's characters and narratives resonate deeply with readers worldwide. Her remarkable ability to seamlessly blend history, humour, and authenticity creates unforgettable stories that both entertain and enlighten.

Now, as Kate Damon, she's ventured into contemporary cozy mysteries with *Jury Duty is Murder*, demonstrating yet again her uncanny knack for crafting compelling tales and memorable protagonists. Her pioneering spirit, seen in the creation of versatile heroines inspired by history's boundary-defying figures, such as Pinkerton detective Kate Warne, continues to inspire readers and aspiring authors alike.

Through her versatility as a storyteller, whether penning tales of love and intrigue or mysteries laced with wit, Kate Damon invites readers into unique worlds that challenge societal norms, celebrate resilience, and embrace both faith and the simple joys of life. In this exclusive interview, you'll gain insight into the creative brilliance behind her works, her fascinating research methods, and the themes that shape her beloved series. This is a conversation you won't want to miss.

In "Calico Spy," you explore a Pinkerton operative's undercover journey—what drew you to blend historical mystery with humor in this final installment of Undercover Ladies?

The humor in the writing was not planned but emerged from the characters, particularly Katie. The primary source of humor is the contrast between her skills as a Pinkerton operative and her difficulties with the duties of a Harvey Girl. She is a skilled Pinkerton operative but has trouble memorizing orders and understanding the Harvey cup-handle code.

Your research on Kate Warne inspired the series—how did uncovering her real-life

Kate Damon shares her creative process, research inspirations, and genre evolution while discussing humour, spiritual depth, and the compelling characters in her bestselling historical romances and cozy mysteries.

Pinkerton role shape Jennifer Layne's character arc in Petticoat Detective?

Women were not allowed to join the police department until 1890. But it was only 1856, when Kate Warne approached Allan Pinkerton for a job. Originally, he thought she was applying for a secretary job, but somehow she convinced him to hire her as a detective. I wanted to create a character similar to Kate Warne—a woman who defied societal norms and wanted to do what no other woman had done.

The iconic shoe-fight scene in your latest novel echoes real childhood antics—how do you balance authenticity and comedy in your Western romances?

The first step is to establish a solid foundation of historical accuracy. This involves thorough research into the time period, including the language, customs, and social norms. It's important to let the humor rise organically from the characters and situations and use it to enhance the story rather than detract from it.

Cowboy Charm School introduces a Texas Ranger with romance—how did you develop Brett Tucker's dynamic relationship with his unconventional heroine?

The initial dynamic between Brett and Kate is shaped by their differing personalities and professional demands. Brett's occupation necessitates a more serious and focused demeanor, while Kate embodies a more carefree and spontaneous approach to life. As Brett and Kate spend more time together and share experiences, their bond deepens, and trust begins to form. They begin to understand and appreciate each other's perspectives, even when they don't agree. Eventually, of course, they fall in love.

Having written more than 46 books, what inspired you most when transitioning from Western historical romance to the contemporary cozy mystery penned under Kate Damon?

I initially intended to write a courtroom romance about a sequestered jury set in the 1800s. I wanted to delve into how being away from family, friends and work for weeks and even months affected juror members. However, after conducting research, I discovered that the first sequestered jury did not occur until 1907, which is quite late for stories set in the Old West. This knowledge led me to abandon the idea—or at least attempt to do so, but the characters kept popping up in my thoughts. Finally, I gave in and began writing the story alongside my

Margaret Brownley's *Cowboy Charm School* is a delightful and humorous Western romance filled with charm, missteps, and swoon-worthy moments. Texas Ranger Brett Tucker's ill-timed intervention spirals into an unexpected love story with bride-to-be Kate Denver. Fans of lighthearted, character-driven tales will adore this heartwarming journey set against a rugged Texan backdrop.

other projects. Much to my surprise, what started out to be a historical soon turned into a contemporary mystery, which I named.

Your quotes often reflect faith and joy in simple moments—how do spiritual themes influence character development across series like Rocky Creek Romance and Brides of Last Chance Ranch?

Spiritual themes serve to shape character development by providing a moral compass, and offering a source of strength, resilience, and purpose. For example, in Cowboy Charm School, the hero's sense of guilt is what drives the narrative. Just as important, spiritual themes also help to foster a sense of community.

In The Outlaw's Daughter, you explore legacy and redemption—what is the most challenging aspect of revisiting the 'Haywire Brides' world with that heavier themeb?

Readers familiar with my books have certain expectations. They expect humor, romance, accurate historical facts and clean entertainment. So whatever I write, I have to be sensitive to what readers know and want from me. So to answer your question, the most significant challenge is to maintain the core appeal of the original series while introducing new elements. This requires careful management of tone, character development, and plot integration. By understanding and respecting these elements, an adaptation can successfully introduce new themes.

What single piece of advice would you offer aspiring authors hoping to craft clean, humorous historical romance or cozy mysteries in today's market?

Don't try chasing the market because it's always changing. However, the thing that never changes is the appeal of well-written stories. So familiarize yourself with what readers want in your chosen genre and give it to them.

> *Don't chase the market; focus on crafting well-written stories."*

Kate Damon

The Brilliant Storyteller Kate Damon, Mastermind Behind Memorable Historical Romances And Intriguing Mysteries

Bringing Scotland's Wild Beauty To Life
S. J. BARRATT
Inspires Young Minds With Eco-Adventures Fueled By Myth, Science And Her Love Of Nature

BY DAN PETERS | LONDON

S. J. Barratt stands as a remarkable force in contemporary children's literature, weaving together threads of ecology, adventure, and myth into tales that both educate and enchant. Based in the picturesque surroundings of Lyon, France, Barratt's life is deeply rooted in sustainable agriculture—a passion that unmistakably infuses her writing with authenticity and a respect for the natural world. Her award-winning series, Living at the Edge of the World, captivates middle-grade readers with its compelling settings, diverse stories, and heartfelt themes—all underscored by her meticulous research and dedication to environmental storytelling.

In this issue of Reader's House, we have the immense pleasure of sharing an illuminating interview with Barratt. Her eco-fiction series, set amidst Scotland's storied landscapes, has not only charmed reviewers but also garnered accolades such as the Silver Medal at BookFest 2024 for diversity in children's books and recognition from the Literary Titan. Her debut novel, Winter, brought forward the enduring ethos of Shetland's crofting culture, while its sequel, Spring, delved deeper into archaeology and Viking legend, leaving readers eager for the upcoming instalment, Summer.

From her exploration of social media's impact through her twin protagonists—Tabitha and Timothy—to her nuanced approach to fostering environmental education in young minds, Barratt's work is both timely and timeless. Her stories encourage readers to see the intricate beauty of the world around them, to tread more lightly upon it, and to embrace curiosity as a driving force for wonder and wisdom. As she prepares to unveil the third chapter of her series, featuring themes of ocean pollution and Selkie legends, we can only expect her narrative tapestry to grow richer still.

Through her words, Barratt demonstrates an unwavering belief in the transformative power of stories—blurring boundaries between cultures, landscapes, and the realms of science and myth. It is an honour to spotlight her voice in this issue and to offer our readers a glimpse into the creative mind behind these extraordinary tales.

How did your experience researching crofting and Shetland's landscapes shape the setting and themes in Living at the Edge of the World – Winter & Spring?

Having worked in agriculture for over 20 years, there are so many aspects of rural life I'd love young readers—and their parents—to better understand. I knew from the start that I wanted the story to be set on a farm, and crofting in Scotland felt like the perfect fit: small-scale, family-run, and deeply rooted in both community and the land.

When I came across Shetland, especially the island of Foula—with its population of just 30 people—I was captivated. It was the ideal backdrop to explore themes of isolation, resilience, and identity. The stark contrast between this remote, rustic way of life and the world of a wannabe influencer from trendy North London gave me a compelling framework for both tension and humor.

S. J. Barratt discusses eco-fiction, Viking legends, social dynamics, and cultural identity in her award-winning Living at the Edge of the World series, blending adventure, education, and environmental themes for middle-grade readers.

Winter garnered awards in 2024—how did recognition influence your approach to Spring, published March 20, 2025?

Winning my first award—a Silver Medal at BookFest—was such a thrill that I proudly featured it on Winter's cover. It gave me a real confidence boost and reinforced that the themes I was exploring resonated with readers.

When writing Spring, I felt encouraged to keep pushing myself creatively while staying true to the heart of the story. I've submitted it to a range of awards, including the North Street Book Prize, which offers valuable feedback—even if you don't win. That insight is invaluable to me.

The awards Winter received confirmed there's an appetite for stories that reflect both cultural diversity and unique landscapes. It's helped shape my direction going forward:

• Silver Medalist, BookFest 2024 — Children's Books: Diversity & Multicultural
• Bronze Medalist, Global Book Awards 2024 — Geography & Culture
• Finalist, Children's Book Excellence Awards 2025

Spring has since received a children's literature award from Literary Titan.

In Spring, the twins uncover a Viking artefact—what inspired you to weave archaeology and legend into a story for ages 9–12?

Many themes in my stories are grounded in real-life events. A few years ago, an islander in Foula digging for peat unearthed woollen fabric dating back to the Vikings. It wasn't a dramatic helmet or sword, but it sparked my imagination. I expanded on that and added a fictional twist to make it exciting for young readers.

I also wove in a simple soil experiment using cotton, to show how organic material breaks down over time—hands-on science that kids can try themselves. Combining real-world science with Norse legend made the writing process fun and educational—even for me!

The contrast between Tabitha's social-media mindset and Timothy's love of nature offers sharp character arcs—how did you develop that sibling dynamic?

I've always loved the dynamic between twins—so similar, yet so different. Tabitha is all about online validation and influencer dreams, while Timothy—"Wiki-Tim"—is grounded in curiosity and nature. His love of facts lets me bring in real information without it feeling forced—if I do it right!

I enjoy engaging with my own online community, but nothing restores the soul like a walk in nature, and I wanted that message to come through. Tabitha's journey isn't about judging social media, but about discovering that face-to-face connection and time outdoors can be even more fulfilling.

Your eco-fiction highlights agro-ecology and peat-bog conservation—how important is environmental education in your storytelling?

Very! I wanted readers to better understand how farming can work with nature. Agro-ecology is all about balance—especially important in crofting, where every bit of land counts. And peatbogs are amazing carbon sinks, so protecting them is crucial.

That said, if you live beside one, cutting peat for heating might still be more sustainable than importing fuel. In Spring, the twins are learning to cut peat when they stumble on the Viking helmet. It was a great opportunity to blend environmental education with adventure.

You're based in France but write about Shetland—how does living abroad affect your connection to Papala and its culture?

Having lived in France for longer than I did in Britain, I often feel caught between cultures—which naturally finds its way into my writing. The sense of not fully belonging is something I explore through Papala's characters and their varied backgrounds. In Winter, the twins—newcomers to the island—meet a Syrian boy, and together they navigate what it means to be different.

I've visited Shetland and Scotland many times and have established a lovely correspondence with a ranger from Foula, who generously reviews my drafts—especially the wildlife and farming details I rely on.

In your Q&A you mention "forcing yourself to write" through writer's block—what's your current writing routine while working on Summer?

I don't really believe in writer's block. I see it more as something to push through by simply getting words on the page. You can rewrite anything—but not a blank page.

I've finished the first draft of Summer, the third book, and I'm giving it some space before editing. I write best in the mornings, usually early when the house is quiet—or even propped up in bed with my laptop before the day begins. It might sound lazy, but it works for me!

Summer explores ocean pollution and the myths of the Selkies—those half-seal, half-human sea folk from Scottish legend. I'm aiming for publication next summer, with time set aside for self-editing, beta readers, professional feedback, and of course illustration work with the talented Jenny Nutbourne.

What one piece of advice would you give aspiring middle-grade authors hoping to blend adventure, ecology, and myth in children's literature?

Let curiosity lead the way. Research deeply, reach out to experts, and stay open to inspiration—whether it comes from a scientific article, a legend, or a single photo. The more curious you are, the richer and more meaningful your story will become.

S. J. Barratt, award-winning storyteller, blending myth, nature, and eco-fiction to inspire young readers through her *Living at the Edge of the World* series.

> *Research deeply, reach out to experts, and stay open to inspiration—curiosity can transform any story into something truly meaningful."*
>
> # S. J. Barratt

Wartime Memories And Historical Depth
ELIZABETH WINTHROP ALSOP
Inspires With Stories of Family, Courage and Imagination

BY DAN PETERS | LONDON

Elizabeth Winthrop Alsop stands as a paragon of literary brilliance, whose body of work spans generations, genres, and hearts alike. Her career, marked by over sixty titles, embodies a unique blend of creativity, emotional depth, and timeless ingenuity. Under her pen name, Elizabeth Winthrop, she has gifted readers an array of narratives ranging from the enchanting fantasy classics *The Castle in the Attic* and *The Battle for the Castle*, to historical fiction masterpieces such as *Counting on Grace*. Her deft ability to breathe life into characters—whether navigating medieval castles, turn-of-the-century mill towns, or their own family memories—is a testament to her nuanced and evocative storytelling.

Her memoir, *Daughter of Spies: Wartime Secrets, Family Lies*, takes readers into the intimate landscape of her own family history, unveiling stories intertwined with espionage, love, addiction, and resilience. This profoundly personal work complements the depth and precision evident in her historical fiction, offering a deeply human exploration of her mother's life as an MI5 agent during World War II and the nuanced complexities of their relationship.

Elizabeth's versatility extends beyond novels to picture books with titles like *Dumpy La Rue* and *The First Christmas Stocking*, each characterised by a whimsical charm delicately balanced with heartfelt themes. Her works for children, celebrated with accolades including the California Young Reader's Medal and the Dorothy Canfield Fisher Award, consistently resonate with young minds and instil values of courage, imagination, and connection.

The forthcoming prequel to *The Castle in the Attic* reflects her knack for weaving multi-dimensional stories, rooted in historical richness yet imbued with magical intrigue. From a wartime beach in 1943 England to the medieval magnificence of a newly constructed castle, her creativity knows no bounds—a reminder that her imagination, like her characters, continues to surprise and enlighten.

As an author who writes across genres and age ranges, Elizabeth Winthrop Alsop remains an inspiring figure for aspiring writers. Her advice—to remain open to life's passing moments and document even the smallest sparks—is a fitting homage to her ability to transform the ordinary into the extraordinary. This interview invites us behind the curtain of a true literary luminary who has given readers works filled with courage, family, whimsy, and magic for decades. Her words beckon us to embrace vulnerability and the boundless possibilities of creative exploration.

How did writing your memoir Daughter of Spies differ emotionally and technically from crafting historical fiction like Counting on Grace and Dear Mr. President?

Character drives my work, be it fiction, historical fiction or memoir. In the case of historical fiction like Counting on Grace and

Elizabeth Winthrop Alsop shares insights on her memoir, historical fiction, fantasy, and picture books while discussing themes of family, courage, and the creative process that fuels her enduring storytelling.

Dear Mr. President, the character comes to me through the research. In the case of my memoir, Daughter of Spies, my mother and I were the two main characters. Her memories and mine led me to the research which allowed me to tell our stories, both separately and intermingled, in greater depth.

What made you decide to focus your memoir on your mother?

My father, Stewart Alsop, was a famous journalist. Books and plays have been written about him, and he wrote his own memoir, Stay of Execution, about facing death after a dire leukemia diagnosis. When my five brothers and I were growing up in the secretive world of Cold War Washington, my mother, a young British war bride, lived in the shadow cast by my father's outsized reputation. None of us ever really knew her, least of all her only daughter. As she began to slip into dementia, I was determined to tell the story of her life as an MI5 decoding agent in London during World War II, the frustrations of her post-war role in America as the wife of a famous man and the mother of six children, and the ways her loneliness and addiction affected me. In the end, as often happens with memoir, I learned as much about myself as I did about my mother.

Having never outlined The Castle in the Attic, how did you navigate plot twists and character arcs without a predetermined structure?

In writing The Castle in the Attic, I learned to let the characters take the lead. Nowadays, I keep what I call a journal of the book and that's where I talk myself through the upcoming scenes and ask myself questions. Can I trap this character in a watery cave with the tide rising? I like the idea, but who will rescue her and how? Outlining books traps me in my earliest scenarios and I begin to serve the outline more than the needs, wants and actions of my characters. When I free them (and myself) from the outline, they speak to me and make moves that surprise me in all the best ways. They come alive for me, and hopefully, for the reader.

What inspired the return to your medieval fantasy world in the upcoming Castle in the Attic prequel centered on Richard?

I finished The Battle for the Castle, the sequel to The Castle in the Attic, seven years after Castle. In re-reading the two books, I realized that there should be an overarching villain, one who sent both the evil wizard Alastor, and the monster rats. What better way to introduce that villain but in a prequel? Mrs. Phillips' brother, Richard, was the reason she had to leave William and return to England, so as the reader had already heard of him, he was the natural focus of the prequel. Daughter of Spies is partially set in England during World War II, so I relished the idea of a character who time travels from 1943 Northumberland where, in the shadow

Elizabeth Winthrop Alsop: Celebrated author of over sixty books, sharing heartfelt tales woven with family, courage, history, and timeless magic.

of a ruined castle, the beaches are mined to repel a German invasion to the exact same spot in 1366 where that same castle has just been erected.

Your picture books, such as The First Christmas Stocking and The Biggest Parade, explore family themes—how do you balance whimsy with deeper emotional resonance?

The picture book form, like a poem, gives the writer lots of room to explore within a tight structure. In most cases you have 28 pages (32 pages minus 4 pages of front matter) to tell your story. You give away half the story to the illustrator so in Shoes, when I wrote, "Shoes for sliding, shoes for hiding, high topped shoes for horseback riding," the illustrator is the one who put my characters on metal horses riding a carousel. The words can inspire a sense of whimsy in the illustrator. Another way to bring in whimsy is to make an animal the central character as I did in The Biggest Parade and its prequel, Dog Show. In those books, Harvey the dog owner, is the foolish one and his basset hound Fred, the wise sidekick. Kids connect with the character they most admire be it a person or a dog so it's possible to introduce tougher emotional subjects in many ways such as using rhymes, puns and unlikely characters, to name a few.

Counting on Grace shines in school curricula—how did you approach writing a historical novel with educational value and compelling narrative?

Counting on Grace was inspired by a photograph that the great child labor photographer, Lewis Hine, took of a small girl working in a Vermont textile factory. When I studied her worried expression, her filthy smock, her bare feet covered in oil, I knew I wanted to tell her story. At that point, I wasn't interested in the actual child, so I created Grace, a 10-year-old girl of French-Canadian descent, forced to work in the mill six days a week. Once again, because I did such deep research on what life was like for those children in the town of North Pownal, Vermont in 1910, the reader and I were both grounded in that place and time which makes for a compelling narrative. Readers Grace's age can easily imagine what life might have been like for them if they had been born in a mill town over 100 years ago.

With over sixty books published, how do you keep your storytelling fresh while revisiting recurring themes like courage, family and magic?

Stories come to me from all directions, both inside from something I've experienced or from outside when for example, I overhear an interesting conversation. As long as I bring an honest emotional perspective to the work, the storytelling stays fresh.

What single piece of advice would you give aspiring authors striving to write across genres and age ranges like you've done?

Stay open to whatever or whomever crosses your path and write it all down, even the bits and pieces that seem inconsequential. They could end up as the core of your next story.

> *As often happens with memoir, I learned as much about myself as I did about my mother."*

Elizabeth W. Alsop

MULTI AWARD-WINING AUTHOR

Enriching Asian Cultural Heritage With Heartfelt Narratives

APPLE AN

Inspires Through Stories That Bridge Cultures And Illuminate Real-Life Resilience Touch Hearts Across The Globe

as told to Ben Alan

Apple An shares her journey from STEM scholar to an award-winning author, blending cultural authenticity, historical research, and personal resilience into memoirs and fiction that inspire readers globally.

Apple An's literary journey is nothing short of remarkable. From her distinguished career as a professor in STEM fields to her emergence as a beacon of storytelling, Apple embodies excellence, creativity, and resilience in every endeavour she undertakes. Her debut memoir, *Las Crosses: An Unwavering Journey to a New Life in America*, not only sheds light on her personal odyssey but also captivates readers with its authenticity and depth. Apple's ability to transform her family's experiences into universally resonant narratives has earned her accolades, placing her among Amazon's bestsellers and cementing her reputation as a literary luminary.

Her subsequent foray into historical fiction with *Mother of Red Mountains: A Novel of a Woman's Journey Through Revolutionary China* further exemplifies her narrative prowess. This deeply moving novel, a tribute to her mother and loving mothers everywhere, underscores Apple's mastery of weaving cultural specificity with universal themes. Garnering multiple awards and becoming a favourite in diverse categories such as Family Saga and Multicultural Fiction, the book stands as a testament to Apple's skill in crafting immersive settings and unforgettable characters. Her personal experiences, resilience, and scientific enquiry into the human condition breathe life into her protagonists, drawing readers into vivid worlds rich with sensory detail and emotional truth.

Not just an author, Apple's contributions transcend the literary domain. Alongside Georgia A. Popoff, she co-edits the *Voices Heard Anthology Series*, providing aspiring writers with a platform to share their stories and perspectives. Her self-help publication, *All-in-One Dotted Journal Notebook*, offers insights into her productive life, reflecting her belief in mindful living and creative discipline.

Apple An's journey from growing up during China's Cultural Revolution to becoming an inspiring voice for cultural understanding is one of unparalleled resolve and artistic brilliance. Her works illuminate the importance of bridging cultural divides, dispelling stereotypes, and cherishing the quiet strength of everyday heroes. It is with great pride that we present this interview with Apple An, whose stories continue to resonate across borders and inspire readers

Continued *on page 30*

STAR INTERVIEW

" Apple An, bestselling author and literary luminary, exemplifies resilience and creativity, crafting stories that resonate with readers across borders.

Photos by Tony Li

Continued *from page 28*

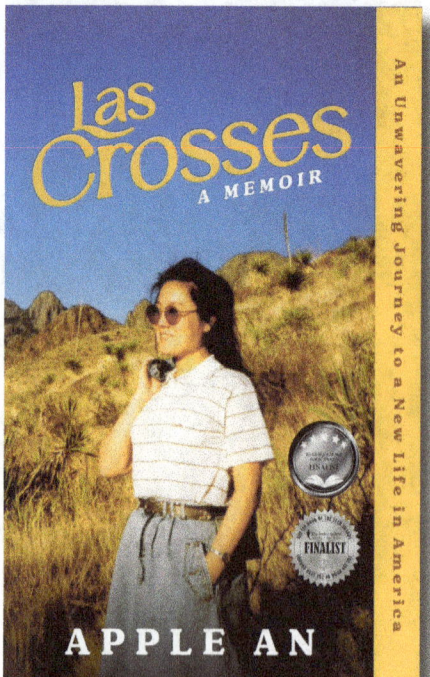

Apple An's memoir Las Crosses: An Unwavering Journey to a New Life in America is a touching and candid recounting of her transition from Beijing to Las Cruces, New Mexico, in the late 1980s. Through evocative storytelling, An unpacks the struggles and triumphs of starting anew in a foreign land, capturing both the personal and cultural nuances of immigration.

The book opens with her arrival in America, vividly describing the chaos of navigating complex airports and stone-faced customs officers, juxtaposed with the riveting sense of hope inspired by the crisp, blue skies of the Southwest. An's observations about the fresh air, unfamiliar landscapes, and cultural adjustments reveal her sharp eye for detail and her ability to translate raw experiences into compelling prose. Her ability to breathe life into seemingly mundane moments is a standout feature of this memoir.

In twelve chapters, An shares anecdotes ranging from humorous—like the struggle to repack dismantled suitcases—to deeply emotional reflections on finding her place in an unknown world. The chapters, such as "Dropped-Noodle Soup" and "Driving to the West," effectively fuse her personal journey with universal themes of resilience, adaptation, and the pursuit of identity. Her genuine voice shines throughout, making the memoir relatable and deeply human.

Recognised as a finalist for several prestigious awards, including the 2023 IAN Book of the Year Awards for "Women's Non-Fiction" and "Multicultural Non-Fiction," Las Crosses is a testament to the author's skill and dedication. This memoir will resonate with readers who appreciate heartfelt narratives of survival and self-discovery amidst life's unpredictabilities.

Las Crosses brings forth the author's unwavering spirit, celebrating the beauty of transformation and the intricacies of what it means to truly belong. It is a must-read for fans of immigrant tales and introspective memoirs.

worldwide. May her distinctive voice and unyielding dedication encourage all who seek to express their truths and enrich humanity through the power of storytelling.

In your most recent book Mother of Red Mountains, what inspired you to explore the specific cultural or historical themes that have clearly resonated with readers?

I have always wanted to tell the stories of myself and my family in China to the five children under my care who grew up in the U.S. When I shared my early drafts with my writing teachers and friends, they made me realize my stories could be interesting to many people who only read limited stories or news pieces about China. I also realized that many stereotypes and misunderstandings about cultures and upbringings have a lot to do with not being able to read rich stories.

After over 30 years as a professor in STEM fields, I found a calling to write about real people I know to enrich Asian cultural heritage and history. I believe such stories can enhance cultural understanding and acceptance among all people, which can make our world a much better place.

While working on my life stories, my mom's stories kept popping up. I felt the urge and even obligation to write this book on her behalf, or to write about her life the way I understood it now, after being a mom myself. Besides showing her and other Chinese women's resilience, I wanted my stories to have a hopeful and positive spin to encourage and inspire readers.

Could you describe your research process for your latest novel and how it informed your character development?

I used online tools to make sure the historical background details were accurate. I approached family members and friends to capture their memories and insights. Some old photos from my mom's collection allowed me to identify unique features and explore them further for historical details.

My long-time training as a scientist prompted me to ask the WHY question out of the large amount of materials and memories. An excellent novel is not just a passive description of what happened. It begs for all the W questions, especially the What, When, Why, and How. As a mom myself, writing this novel was a personal healing process where disjointed events and scenes I was familiar with from my youth made great sense now. This allowed me to see my mom's life in a new light and appreciate what she had endured even more. Only after this could I bring her to life and make her the heroine in the book.

STAR INTERVIEW

Apple's transformation from STEM professor to bestselling author.

Her memoir sheds light on immigrant experiences with depth and authenticity.

Historical fiction inspired by her mother's resilience during China's Revolution.

Upcoming historical novel, Daughter of Blue City, building on Mother of Red Mountains.

Continued *on page 32*

STAR INTERVIEW

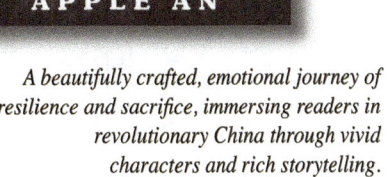

A beautifully crafted, emotional journey of resilience and sacrifice, immersing readers in revolutionary China through vivid characters and rich storytelling.

A brilliantly versatile journal that merges organisation, creativity, and mindfulness, empowering users to master productivity while fostering personal growth.

Apple An's authentic stories and poignant themes illuminate resilience, bridging cultural divides with brilliance and inspiring readers worldwide.

APPLE AN

MULTI AWARD-WINNING AUTHOR

Apple grew up during China's Cultural Revolution and came to the U.S. in 1989 in her 20s. Her biggest achievement was to be a mom and guardian of five children. She writes, with her pen name Apple An, short stories, memoirs, and historical novels about her life and those of people she knows. Her writing goal is to enrich Asian cultural heritage and history and to enhance cultural understanding and acceptance among all people.

In 2023, Apple published her debut book,

Mother of Red Mountains is a sweeping and poignant historical novel that captures the resilience of a woman navigating the tumultuous landscape of revolutionary China. Framed against the backdrop of the Cultural Revolution and mid-20th century societal challenges, the story follows Jun, a gifted civil engineer whose life is marked by ambition, sacrifice, and indomitable courage.

Apple An's writing is evocative, blending vivid depictions of China's landscapes and culture with the personal and political struggles of its characters. Jun's transformation from a child fostering hopes in her father's shop to a high-achieving career woman is equal parts inspiring and heartbreaking. Yet, the intrusion of the Red Guards during the Cultural Revolution thrusts her into a protective maternal role, forcing her to prioritise her daughters' survival above her aspirations.

An excels in weaving rich historical detail with a narrative that is deeply personal, offering readers both a glimpse into the socio-political upheaval of revolutionary China and an emotionally resonant tale of motherhood, identity, and resilience. The novel's insights into human tenacity make it universally relatable.

Gripping and beautifully crafted, *Mother of Red Mountains* is a triumph that honours untold women's stories—an unforgettable saga worthy of its accolades.

Las Crosses, a memoir of the first eight months after she arrived in America from Beijing. It received 2nd and 3rd places and was a finalist for book awards in categories of memoirs, women's non-fiction, multicultural non-fiction, and travel.

In 2024, Apple released her first historical novel, Mother of Red Mountains, based on actual events and people. The book won awards from eight award agencies in categories of multicultural fiction, historical fiction, family saga, best first novel, and best adult book.

The In twelve chapters *All-in-One Dotted Journal NotebookIn twelve chapters* by Apple An is a versatile tool tailored for those juggling busy, multifaceted lives. Marketed as a planner, organiser, tracker, and creative space, it delivers impressively on its promise to support productivity and mindfulness. The dotted layout is ideal for customisation, giving users the freedom to design their own templates, whether for daily planning, habit tracking, or creative doodling.

One of its standout features is the thoughtful structure combined with flexibility. The upfront examples and guidance are genuinely helpful for beginners, offering inspiration without feeling overly prescriptive. The book's ability to encompass everything from goal-setting and accountability to managing hobbies, health, or even seasonal tasks is truly remarkable.

However, it may feel overwhelming for those unfamiliar with bullet journalling or for individuals who prefer a more straightforward, plug-and-play planner. It requires an investment of time and creativity to tailor it to your specific needs, which won't suit everyone.

This robust journal is best suited to individuals looking for an all-encompassing organisational tool with room for personalisation. With its focus on mindfulness and balanced living, it's an excellent choice for readers ready to invest in organising their lives while sparking creativity.

Apple designed a journal notebook to assist her in living a busy, productive, and mindful life. She published it as a self-help book to benefit others. Apple also co-edits the Voices Anthology Series, which includes contributions from writers who attended The Writer's Voice classes and workshops.

Apple has been a professor of STEM fields at Syracuse University since 1995. She is a USTA-rated tennis player and an award-winning amateur ballroom dancer. In her spare time, she enjoys organic gardening, hiking, traveling, movies, concerts, books, and cultural events.

Reader's House || 31

← **Continued** *from page 30*

Here are a few photos that inspired the development of the characters and their lives in Part 1 of the book.

The protagonist Jun started school at 14 to help her sister Xia stay in school. See Chapter 5 Mr. Liu's Wishes. cf. 1949, Chifeng.

After changing her name for the first time to be gender neutral, Jun was about to leave her hometown to start a vocational school to be financially independent. See Chapter 11 Far Away. c.f. 1956, Chifeng.

Your popular work features strong, diverse protagonists—how did your personal experiences influence their portrayal?

The important women in my life, my mom, aunt, parental grandma, and sister, all exhibited courage, grit, and overall, a quiet strength that I didn't see in men in my life. Yet, they hardly received much recognition and appreciation.

Being constantly bullied and having faced domestic violence while growing up and being publicly or silently discriminated against during my adult life, I have a lot to draw to make the characters and scenes relatable.

You utilise vivid sensory detail—how do you craft such immersive settings that engage readers fully?

When I wrote a scene, I often saw it unfolding in front of me as if it was a movie or play, and I was the camera. That required the writing to make logical senseand allow the audience to see, hear, and smell. It was as if the reader were next to the main characters inside the scene.

How did your background influence the narrative voice in your most recent bestseller?

I was born and grew up in China and came to the U.S. at 26 to work on my doctoral degree. Although I didn't live through the period the book covered, from 1946 to 1966, my research and my mom's storytelling transferred me back to the time, which helped me understand what happened and how people felt.

What challenges did you face in blending genre conventions with your unique storytelling style?

This book is my first novel. There was a lot of learning to write fiction. I studied many craft books about writing novels and screenplays to understandvarious aspects. My top notable craft books are Story by McKee, Story Engineering by Brooks, The Emotional Craft of Fiction by Maass, and The Trope Thesaurus by Hilt. To learn about the specifics of historical fiction, I listened to audio booksbymanyhighly acclaimed authors. A few of my favorite books are The Pecan Man by Selleck, The Bonesetter's Daughter by Tan, and Kristin Hannah's The Great Alone, The Four Winds, and The Women.

Your work has evidently struck a chord globally—how do you balance universal themes with cultural specificity?

Despite the differences among people, we are all human inside. We all have emotions, struggles, and good and bad times. The best way to connect with readers is to be truthful and authentic.

What are you working on now?

My second historical novel, Daughter of Blue City, is to be released in the fall of 2025. Although a stand-alone book, it picks up from where Mother of Red Mountains left and covers the family's life from 1966 to 1980. It paints the real-life picture from the view of Lianlian, Jun's first born who witnessed and remembered the violence at 3 during the onset of China's Cultural Revolution in 1966. The backdrop of the story is China's tremendous change during these years that laid the foundation for what China is now.

What key piece of advice would you offer aspiring authors wanting to emulate your success and distinctive voice?

Literary fiction has its own rules and norms, very different from academic writing and other intellectual exercises. Mastering these rules and norms is very important. But that is not enough: an author needs to find his or her voice.

I didn't emulate anyone's voice and wouldn't advise any aspiring authors to do the same. I wanted to tell my story inways I felt natural to me. Finding my voice was a process. I knew what I wanted to write about and what emotional and cognitive effects I hoped to generate. But I didn't know if my writing delivered the intended effects. Sharing my drafts with others was tremendously helpful●

Jun didn't get along with her sister-in-law, who had no education and believed the only role of a married woman was to raise children. This was before she took Xia to live in a schoolroom after her father passed away. See Chapter 6 Home No More. c.f. 1952, Chifeng.

Exploring the World of BDSM Romance with Annabel Joseph

Annabel Joseph discusses her passion for BDSM romance, character authenticity, personal inspiration, and balancing fantasy with responsibility while sharing highlights of her unique narratives and award-winning works.

Annabel Joseph, a New York Times and USA Today bestselling author, is celebrated for her emotionally charged exploration of BDSM and romance. Her novels, which primarily delve into contemporary settings, have earned a passionate following among readers who crave intensity combined with richly developed characters. Joseph's talent for portraying dominant-submissive relationships with authenticity and nuance elevates her work above traditional romance, creating stories that resonate deeply with audiences.

Joseph's ability to bring depth and realism to her characters stems from her dedication to research and her own personal familiarity with the themes she writes about. *"Great BDSM relationships are like a dance, and I find that dance, that push and pull, extremely exciting to put on the page,"* she shared in her interview with Mosaic Digest. For Joseph, exploring dominance and submission isn't merely about writing erotica; it's about uncovering the complex emotions and connections that can emerge within power dynamics. This commitment to authenticity represents her respect for both the lifestyle and the audience who connect with her work's emotional truths.

Character development is another hallmark of her writing. With a background in creative writing, Joseph has honed the craft of making flawed, multifaceted characters who endear themselves to readers. Whether it's through intense dialogue, steamy scenes, or internal struggles, her stories are layered with meaning. *"Readers need all the senses: the sights, the sounds, the sensations. I also try to weave in multiple layers of connection and meaning to increase the hotness factor,"* she explained. Joseph finds excitement in surprising herself as she develops characters or scenes, leading to magical moments in her novels that captivate her audience.

Much of Joseph's work challenges societal norms by diving into the psychology of relationships. She isn't shy away from exploring taboo subjects or pushing boundaries in her storytelling. For the author, these challenges are deeply personal. *"My experiences and references shape a lot of what I put on the page,"* she said, admitting that many of her characters are inspired by people she has admired—or simply observed—in real life. Whether knowingly or unknowingly, these individuals become integral to Joseph's fictional worlds.

Balancing authenticity and fantasy is a delicate act, particularly in the BDSM romance genre. Joseph is careful to offer disclaimers to her readers, clarifying that her novels depict fantasies rather than real-world practices. *"The key is for readers to know the difference between fantasy and real life,"* she emphasized. Nonetheless, she acknowledges the transformative power of her stories, recounting letters from fans who credit her books with reawakening intimacy in their relationships. These moments are proof of how deeply her writing resonates with readers on both an emotional and personal level.

After years in the industry, Joseph has amassed an extensive backlist. While grateful for the journey, she admits she cringes at her earliest works. *"They're so raw, but I also love them for that reason,"* she said. She gifted her readers with surprising genre explorations, including historical-kink series and novellas, to keep her creativity flowing. Of all her works, her *Cirque Masters* series occupies a special place in her heart. *"It was a pure joy to write,"* she revealed, describing how the characters and themes came vividly to life for her. The series kicks off with *Cirque de Minuit*, a must-read for fans of Joseph's work. Another standout title is *Torment Me*, an award-winning book that earned her the Golden Flogger, a recognition of excellence in BDSM writing.

Outside of her writing world, Joseph resides in Atlanta, Georgia, with her family and two energetic terriers. She spends her free time indulging in show tunes, daydreaming, and tending to her ferns. Annabel also publishes non-BDSM romance under the pen name Molly Joseph, showcasing her versatility as an author.

For readers willing to explore raw emotions, sensuality, and the intricate dance of dominance and submission, Annabel Joseph's novels offer unparalleled storytelling. She not only crafts unforgettable characters but also sheds light on the deeper connections that make romance truly transformative. Her stories prove that sometimes, pushing boundaries leads to unforgettable and meaningful experiences.

From Raw Beginnings To Award-Winning Tales

Annabel Joseph's emotionally rich storytelling, authentic character development, and bold exploration of BDSM themes make her a genre-defining author.

"My writing builds on experiences or fantasies I've had, or stories that have been shared with me."

Annabel Joseph

Overcoming Challenges While Creating Imaginative Worlds

Author Michael Thal discusses his profound narratives, blending personal experience with fiction, overcoming deafness, and inspiring readers through enchanting works like the Koolura Series, Goodbye Tchaikovsky, and *The Lip Reader*.

MICHAEL THAL
Shares His Inspiring Journey and Captivating Stories Through Diverse Genres

"The best way to show a person's inner nature is not what they say, but what they do."

Editor's Desk | London

Michael Thal is a literary treasure whose powerful storytelling and diverse narratives have touched readers of all ages. As the mastermind behind six captivating novels, including *Goodbye Tchaikovsky*, *The Abduction of Joshua Bloom*, and the enchanting Koolura Series—*The Legend of Koolura*, *Koolura and the Mystery at Camp Saddleback*, and *Koolura and the Mayans*—Michael has proven himself a writer capable of weaving imagination with heartfelt authenticity. His works resonate deeply, offering a remarkable blend of adventure, inspiration, and meaningful life lessons.

Having faced the life-changing challenge of losing his hearing at the age of 50, Michael's resilience and creative spirit stand as a testament to his strength and determination. Not only has he reinvented himself as an accomplished author after a successful teaching career, but he's also become a storyteller who draws from his personal experiences to bring authenticity and emotional depth to his characters. His portrayal of profound themes—whether through a deaf musician's journey in *Good-

bye, Tchaikovsky, the extraordinary psychic adventures of Koolura, or the moving narrative of a deaf woman in *The Lip Reader*—elevates his work to a relatable and inspirational level.

Michael's unique ability to explore a variety of genres, from sci-fi to middle-grade fantasy, while remaining deeply connected to human emotions and experiences, makes his writing both versatile and timeless. As readers, we are fortunate to journey through the universes he creates, finding not only entertainment but also profound messages on perseverance, kindness, and personal growth. Michael Thal's remarkable ability to transform life's challenges into art is truly a gift to the literary world. We are honoured to share this insightful interview with him, offering readers a glimpse into the mind of a writer whose stories continue to inspire.

What inspired you to write The Abduction of Joshua Bloom, and how did you develop such a unique interplanetary narrative?

When I was 27 years old, I had a dream in which I was abducted by aliens and sent to another world. I woke in the middle of the night, wrote the dream down, and went back to sleep. From those notes I wrote a short story and showed it to a friend who said, "This looks like an outline for a book."

> Michael Thal is a masterful storyteller whose resilience and creativity inspire readers while delivering heartfelt, imaginative narratives across genres.

How much of your personal experience with hearing loss influenced your portrayal of David in Goodbye, Tchaikovsky?

Imagine waking up one morning deaf. A virus, overnight, robbed me of my hearing. I've controlled my deafness by embracing it. For example, I'm near fluent in American Sign Language and President of Temple Beth Solomon of the Deaf. When I wrote Goodbye, Tchaikovsky, it was my way of figuring out what life would have been like for me if I lost my hearing at 12 rather than 44.

The Koolura series features a young girl with psychic powers—what message were you hoping to convey to younger readers through her journey?

I truly believe all of us have the same purpose in life: Helping each other. Koolura is kind to her friends, even the obnoxious ones like Linda. I hope readers can read between the lines and get that message.

In The Lip Reader, you portray the life of a deaf woman navigating immense challenges. How did you balance factual inspiration with fictional storytelling?

The Lip Reader is the fictional account of my wife's life. Before she died of cancer in 2015, she told me many stories about growing up in Iran as a deaf Jew. It wasn't easy, but Jila persevered. I took the facts she told me, like a trip with family to Europe and Israel, and I filled in the gaps with my imagination.

What kind of research went into writing A Long Journey to a New Home, particularly in portraying 19th-century Norwegian immigrants?

I didn't write that book. I told Amazon, but they don't listen very well.

You've written across various genres—sci-fi, middle-grade fantasy—what drives you to explore such diverse themes?

I wrote the Koolura books because my daughter refused to read. I suggested to the then 11-year-old, "Would you read a book with a character having psychic powers?" She agreed, and I wrote the books. I was motivated to write Abduction from a dream, and Goodbye and Lip Reader were written out of real-life events. I write what interests me and what's affecting me at the moment. For example, right now I'm taking notes for a book about my dog, Scribble. She's 13 years old, so I know the clock is ticking. I'm keeping a log of her behavior to turn into a book once she passes. I'll need that writing time to help me through dealing with her loss.

Has becoming deaf later in life changed how you approach character development or dialogue in your writing?

I didn't become a full-time writer until my hearing loss. After I lost my hearing, I began noticing non-verbal communication, body language, and show that in my writing. In American Sign Language the main idea is getting to the point immediately. I show that, especially with the Deaf characters. The best way to show a person's inner nature is not what they say, but what they do. That also holds readers' attention.

What advice would you give to aspiring authors, especially those facing personal hardships or unique challenges?

I think aspiring writers facing challenges should write about those hardships. Describe the disability, how it affects you, and how you feel about it. Keep a journal. Then, when the time is right, write about it.

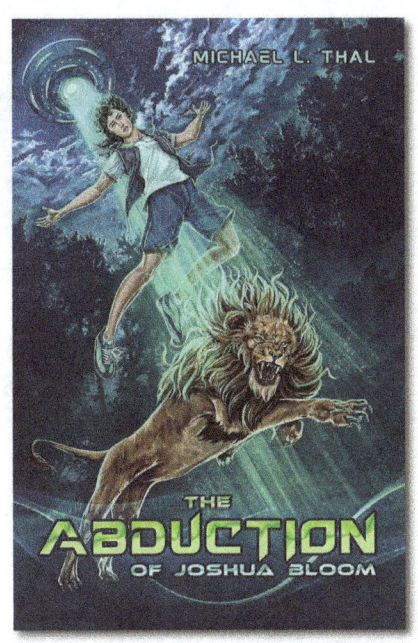

> Michael Thal's *The Abduction of Joshua Bloom* is a mesmerising space opera filled with adventure, ethics, and captivating worlds. With time travel, alien politics, and richly imagined planets, this sci-fi gem offers thought-provoking themes alongside thrilling escapades, making it a must-read for fans of imaginative, interstellar storytelling. A truly unforgettable journey!

Stories, Streets, and Strength in It Was Her New York

C.O. Moed reflects on her memoir, New York roots, and the rhythm of resilience in a voice shaped by laughter, loss, and love.

CO MOED
Shares the Heartbeat of Her City Through Stories That Sing

"That Lower East Side personality and accent has a rhythm unlike any other part of New York."

Editor's Desk | London

Co Moed brings the raw pulse of New York's Lower East Side to the page with a voice that's as unflinching as it is intimate. A streetwise storyteller with a background steeped in music, photography and performance, she captures life's humour, grit, heartbreak and resilience with sharp clarity and a lyrical rhythm all her own. Her debut memoir It Was Her New York – a BookLife Editor's Pick and winner of the Firebird Book Award Judges' Pick – is a stirring collection of true stories and snapshots drawn from her life as a queer woman navigating family, grief, and the city she calls home. In this conversation, Moed reflects on the cultural fusion of her neighbourhood, the irreverent humour that shaped her storytelling, and the process of distilling 1,400 blog entries into a resonant memoir. She also shares insight into her upcoming works, her love of photography, and the strength it takes – both emotional and physical – to lift stories off the ground and into the world.

How did your upbringing on New York's Lower East Side influence the themes and narratives in "It Was Her New York"?

When I meet strangers on the subway or at bus stops and we start talking (as native New Yorkers often do) if we are from the Lower East Side we immediately recognize one another– there is a no bullshit, just a direct, in-your-face-you-need-my-help, street-smart, moxy/sassy quality. That Lower East Side personality and accent has a rhythm unlike any other part of New York because we had (and still have to some degree) all these different communities mushed together on the street – I wrote HER NEW YORK from that street. It's how I talk when I am at my most relaxed and at my most pissed off – down to the bone.

In "It Was Her New York," you blend humor with poignant reflections. How do you balance these elements to engage readers?

Maybe being raised on the Marx Brothers movies had something to do with it? But, honestly, I wasn't trying. That's just how I experienced and communicate things. Definitely on the Lower East Side there is an irreverence about everything – you did not dare take yourself too seriously. No matter how bad circumstances were or if you won the lottery, someone had something to say about it that would make everyone crack up.

Your memoir intertwines personal stories with broader cultural observations. How do you decide which personal anecdotes to include?

I was raised under Florence's piano and I read music before I read English, so everything was and is musical to me. When I started putting HER NEW YORK together from 1400 stories I had posted on a blog, I had an arc/a structure of about 100+ stories about life as Florence got sick and died and going on after she died. All the while, I was constantly seeking "home" as a place to land, to feel safe and recognizable, if only to myself.

New York is a city of mass transit, taxis and walking. The more I put together HER NEW YORK, the more it became the stories of trips I took every day as I went from Florence's home to work to the pharmacy to the park to the subway to the doctor's office. To bring it all together, I lined each story up on index cards. This allowed me to "listen" to the music of how one story flowed into the next and how that home and that walk to home emerged.

"It Was Her New York" has received critical acclaim, including the Firebird Book Award Judge's Pick and BookLife Editor Pick and Distinguished Feature, Independent Press Awards – LGBTQ Nonfiction. How has this recognition impacted your writing journey?

You mean besides my suspicion that some fellow writers now treat me with a bit more respect? It was amazing and very healing to be seen and heard through my work – to be affirmed that my writing didn't suck and I wasn't out of my mind to attempt such a feat. The book competition awards and interviews helped banish lots of those doubts. But it was more than that. I lift weights and the first time I deadlifted 100 pounds (about 45 kg) I cried because I experienced for the first time how strong and capable I was. Putting IT WAS HER NEW YORK out into the world was like lifting that weight. I found out not only what I was capable of, but how important and affirming the stories in the book were to readers.

Your upcoming work, "Home Sweet Home," focuses on photographs of familiar places. How do you use photography to complement your storytelling?

I like pictures. I had a hard time learning to read English and pictures really helped tell me the stories all around me; they explained the world around me. So, when I write, a lot of it is me describing a picture. And when I take a picture, I hear a story in my head.

Your upcoming work, "The Consequences of Penises and Other Unexpected Moments" suggests a candid approach. What inspired you to explore these themes in your writing?

I identify as Queer, so dating men and their penises was a bit unexpected. And what else does a writer do but write about what is going on? So, the collection has some great writing about terrible relationships and some great writing about great relationships like falling for my husband, which has been a much different and much more fun relationship than past ones.

As an author who has navigated both personal and professional writing, what advice would you offer to emerging writers seeking authenticity in their work?

I approach writing like an athlete approaches training. It's a daily grind of repetitive actions, where you succeed and where you fail. All that effort results in words on the page that work. Like the weights I lift, I am lifting that pen over and over and over again and filling pages with crap (so much crap) and then rewriting and rewriting until suddenly something goes WHOOSH and it lifts off the page into OH YEAH!

If you are just starting out, I highly recommend The Artist's Way by Judith Cameron. It built my daily writing muscles and solidified my sense of my right to write. The more I worked that way the more I recognized my own unique voice the more I recognized the people/teachers/mentors/fellow writers there to support me and cheer me on. And the more that unfolded the more I knew who to avoid when sharing my work.

Let's get real: fellow writers, mentors and teachers are like boyfriends and girlfriends. They are either on your side and want you to succeed or they are idiots who come on like they know shit. Find the ones who celebrate your wins, cheer you on despite your failures and support your dreams. And whatever you do, NEVER GIVE UP.

> *A powerful debut full of grit, humour and heart—Moed's voice is unforgettable and her stories deeply human.*

> *It Was Her New York is a poignant memoir of love, loss, and identity, blending essays and photographs to explore caregiving, dementia, queer identity, and a vanishing New York. CO Moed reflects on her mother's decline and their shared past in a changing neighbourhood with humour, heart, and honesty.*

EDITOR'S CHOICE

NOVEL • STORY • LITERATURE

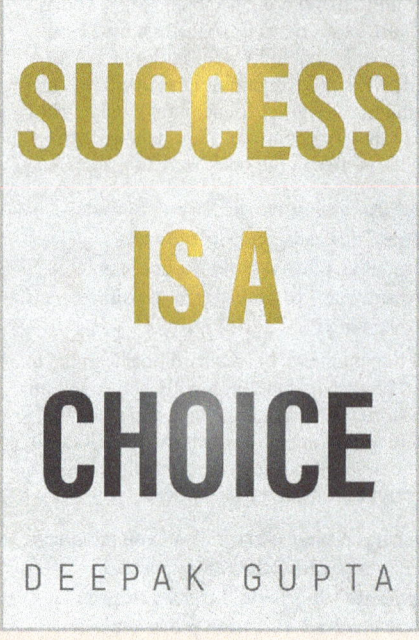

RULE OF FIRE
by Autumn M. Birt

SUCCESS IS A CHOICE
by Deepak Gupta

ICE CAP
by Joan Epp

A captivating adventure with rich world-building, dynamic characters, and thrilling magic. Rule of Fire masterfully blends action, intrigue, and emotional depth.

Insightful, inspiring, and deeply practical—Success is a Choice offers a transformative perspective on personal growth and professional success.

Ice Cap is a charming, heartwarming story with delightful illustrations, spreading kindness, joy, and winter magic for children.

Apple An's memoir Las Crosses: An Unwavering Journey to a New Life in America is a touching and candid recounting of her transition from Beijing to Las Cruces, New Mexico, in the late 1980s. Through evocative storytelling, An unpacks the struggles and triumphs of starting anew in a foreign land, capturing both the personal and cultural nuances of immigration.

The book opens with her arrival in America, vividly describing the chaos of navigating complex airports and stone-faced customs officers, juxtaposed with the riveting sense of hope inspired by the crisp, blue skies of the Southwest. An's observations about the fresh air, unfamiliar landscapes, and cultural adjustments reveal her sharp eye for detail and her ability to translate raw experiences into compelling prose. Her ability to breathe life into seemingly mundane moments is a standout feature of this memoir.

In fifteen chapters, An shares anecdotes ranging from humorous—like the struggle to repack dismantled suitcases—to deeply emotional reflections on finding her place in an unknown world. The chapters, such as "Dropped-Noodle Soup" and "Driving to the West," effectively fuse her personal journey with universal themes of resilience, adaptation, and the pursuit of identity. Her genuine voice shines throughout, making the memoir relatable and deeply human.

Recognised as a finalist for several prestigious awards, including the 2023 IAN Book of the Year Awards for "Women's Non-Fiction" and "Multicultural Non-Fiction," Las Crosses is a testament to the author's skill and dedication. This memoir will resonate with readers who appreciate heartfelt narratives of survival and self-discovery amidst life's unpredictability.

Las Crosses brings forth the author's unwavering spirit, celebrating the beauty of transformation and the intricacies of what it means to truly belong. It is a must-read for fans of immigrant tales and introspective memoirs.

Success is a Choice by Deepak Gupta is a refreshing and thought-provoking take on the self-help genre. Presented through a fictional lens, the story follows Dan Webber, a disheartened executive navigating the frustrations of corporate stagnation. His journey takes a turn when he seeks guidance from Ron Falcon, his younger, more successful boss. What unfolds is a series of conversations that go beyond simple mentorship, offering readers a deeper dive into the philosophies and mindsets that underpin true success.

Gupta cleverly uses narrative to illustrate practical insights, making the book highly relatable and engaging. Instead of the usual bullet-pointed advice, the author weaves his fifty years of business acumen into a compelling storyline that highlights both the psychological barriers and transformative shifts needed to excel.

The book stands out for its blend of corporate realism, spiritual wisdom, and sociological depth. It doesn't merely preach success—it explores how our beliefs, relationships, and self-perceptions shape our paths. Gupta's writing is clear and accessible, yet layered enough to invite reflection, making it suitable for professionals at any stage of their careers.

Though compact in length, the book leaves a lasting impact. It challenges readers to rethink the habits and assumptions that may be quietly sabotaging their progress. More importantly, it empowers them with a simple but powerful message: success is not handed down—it is chosen.

Highly recommended for those seeking more than just career advancement, but a genuine shift in perspective.

Ice Cap by Joan Epp is a heartwarming and delightful tale that captures the magic of winter through the eyes of a snowman with a big heart. The story follows Ice Cap, a fun-loving snowman who springs to life every winter, spreading kindness and joy wherever he goes. With his cool sunglasses, a magical hat, and a heart full of love, Ice Cap brings a unique charm to the chilly season.

The rhyming text flows smoothly, making it an enjoyable read for young children, while the whimsical illustrations by Claire Sedovic complement the playful tone of the story. Whether he's snowboarding, playing games, or building ice castles, Ice Cap's adventures are full of fun and creativity, all with a focus on spreading kindness and making beautiful memories with friends.

Ideal for children aged 3-7, "Ice Cap" is more than just a seasonal story; it's a celebration of friendship, generosity, and the joy of winter. Its lyrical narrative and delightful illustrations make it a perfect addition to any home library, sure to become a favourite at holiday time and beyond.

Joan Epp's debut is a beautifully crafted picture book that will warm the hearts of both children and adults alike, even on the coldest of days. If you're looking for a winter read that's both enchanting and uplifting, "Ice Cap" is a wonderful choice.

NOVEL • STORY • LITERATURE   EDITOR'S CHOICE

THE LEGEND OF ATLANTIS AND THE SCIENCE OF GEOLOGY
by Joseph O'Donoghue

An intellectually stimulating exploration, blending geology and mythology, offering fresh insights into the Atlantis legend with a balanced, open-minded approach.

The Legend of Atlantis and The Science of Geology: Atlantis and Catastrophe: Myth or Reality? by Joseph O'Donoghue offers a compelling and thought-provoking exploration of the Atlantis legend from a scientific perspective. As the first volume in a series, the book combines geological analysis with mythological investigation, presenting a balanced and open-minded approach to a topic often dismissed by mainstream academia.

O'Donoghue, a qualified geologist, challenges the conventional uniformitarian view of geology, suggesting that modern theories may not fully account for the possibility of catastrophic events, such as the destruction of Atlantis. His academic background allows for a unique treatment of the legend, presenting it not as mere myth but as a historical event that could have been shaped by geological phenomena.

The book is thorough in its examination of both ancient and modern views on Atlantis, providing a detailed survey of scholarly opinions, its language and structure, and the historical context of Plato's writings. O'Donoghue also expands the discussion to other global flood and catastrophe myths, offering insights through the lens of geomythology.

For those interested in exploring the intersection of mythology and geology, this book provides a refreshing take on a long-debated mystery. While the author does not definitively claim the reality of Atlantis, he makes a strong case for re-evaluating the geological record and the ancient stories that have often been disregarded.

In summary, *Atlantis and Catastrophe* is an engaging and intellectually stimulating read for anyone curious about the mysteries of the past and the science behind them.

THE CONTENTMENT DIVIDEND
by Michael Goddart

Profound, enlightening, and transformative—The Contentment Dividend offers deep spiritual wisdom, guiding readers toward inner peace, self-discovery, and divine connection.

Michael Goddart's *The Contentment Dividend* offers a contemplative and introspective journey for those seeking spiritual enlightenment and inner peace. Through forty-nine carefully crafted meditations, the book invites readers to quiet the mind's relentless chatter and connect with their higher self. Drawing on decades of study and spiritual practice, Goddart provides a guide for self-discovery and alignment with divine truths.

One of the book's strengths lies in its accessibility. While spiritual texts can often feel dense or overly complex, Goddart presents his meditations in a way that encourages curiosity and reflection. The titles of some meditations may seem cryptic at first, but rather than being off-putting, they serve as an invitation to deeper exploration. His approach is both personal and universal, making the book suitable for seasoned spiritual seekers and those new to meditation alike.

The emphasis on distinguishing between the lower and higher mind is particularly compelling. Goddart illustrates how our habitual thoughts and ego-driven tendencies often cloud our path to contentment. By engaging with the meditations, readers are encouraged to cultivate receptivity to grace and experience a shift in how they navigate life's challenges.

While *The Contentment Dividend* is rooted in the teachings of realised Masters and Saints, it remains practical rather than dogmatic. It is a book to be revisited, each reading offering new insights and deepening one's spiritual understanding. Thought-provoking and uplifting, this is a valuable companion for anyone on the path to self-realisation.

THE BILLIONAIRE'S CONSPIRACY
by MJ Javani

A captivating, fast-paced thriller with intricate plotting, strong characters, and relentless action—MJ Javani delivers an exhilarating reading experience.

The Billionaire's Conspiracy by MJ Javani is a fast-paced and thrilling addition to the Janusz Soltani series. This third instalment catapults readers into a world of high-stakes conspiracy, political intrigue, and relentless action. Javani masterfully crafts a narrative that's both gripping and suspenseful, with twists and turns that keep the reader hooked from start to finish.

The story revolves around Janusz Soltani, a top operative in a private intelligence company, Unit 81, as he uncovers a web of deceit involving a ruthless billionaire and a group of anarchists plotting an attack on the White House. As tensions rise and secrets unravel, Soltani is faced with the horrifying kidnapping of his wife, leading to a desperate race against time to save her.

Javani's writing is sharp and immersive, with well-drawn characters and an engaging plot that moves quickly without losing its depth. The action scenes are particularly well-executed, and the stakes feel genuinely high, making the book a real page-turner for fans of political thrillers.

Though the premise and pace are strong, the book occasionally leans into predictability, especially for those familiar with the genre. However, this doesn't detract from the overall enjoyment, and fans of authors like Ludlum, Flynn, and Thor will certainly appreciate this thrilling ride. *The Billionaire's Conspiracy* is a solid conclusion to the series, providing an exhilarating and satisfying read.

EDITOR'S CHOICE

NOVEL • STORY • LITERATURE

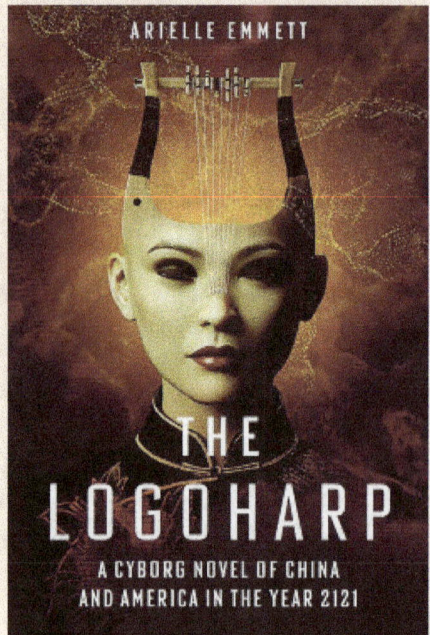
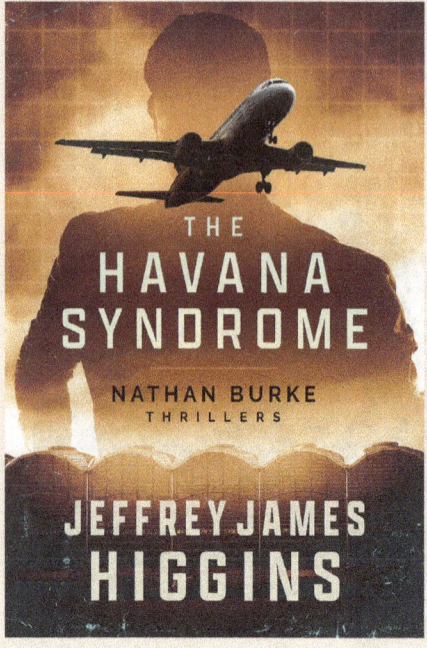

THE LOGOHARP
by *Arielle Emmett*

THE HAVANA SYNDROME
by *Jeffrey James Higgins*

MONOLOGUES FOR KIDS AND TWEENS
by *Mike Kimmel*

Arielle Emmett delivers a bold, thought-provoking debut—brilliantly imaginative, emotionally resonant, and richly layered with futuristic and political depth.

An exhilarating blend of emotion and action, Higgins delivers a thrilling narrative that keeps readers on the edge of their seats.

A brilliant, heartfelt collection that empowers young actors with meaningful, relatable monologues crafted to inspire, educate, and entertain. Truly exceptional.

Arielle Emmett's *The Logoharp* is a dazzlingly inventive, genre-defying cyberpunk novel set in a chilling vision of the year 2121. In this richly imaginative and politically charged future, we meet Naomi—a half-human, half-cyborg Reverse Journalist employed by the Chinese state. Her job is not to report events as they unfold, but to foresee and script the probable future, ensuring the regime stays one step ahead of chaos.

Naomi's tool, the Logoharp, is a mysterious, almost mystical device that transmits instructions in all world languages, guiding her actions and shaping the very fabric of reality. Yet when her past collides with her future in the form of a brilliant architect and former lover, Naomi begins to question her programming—and her humanity.

Emmett's narrative is intellectually daring and laced with sharp commentary on surveillance, state control, eugenics, and identity. The world-building is intricate and immersive, drawing from both ancient Chinese tradition and high-tech dystopian aesthetics. Naomi, as a heroine, is strikingly original—beguiling, deeply flawed, and profoundly sympathetic.

What sets *The Logoharp* apart is its fusion of lyrical prose, philosophical depth, and narrative experimentation. This is not a fast-paced thriller, but a cerebral, emotionally resonant exploration of what it means to resist when the future itself is pre-written.

Bold, provocative, and richly imaginative, *The Logoharp* stands as a vital entry in the canon of speculative fiction, drawing comparisons to Orwell, Gibson, and Bacigalupi, while carving out a voice entirely its own.

A remarkable debut that lingers long after the final page.

In the gripping first instalment of the Nathan Burke Thrillers, Jeffrey James Higgins delivers a pulse-pounding narrative that expertly intertwines personal stakes with global espionage. FBI Agent Nathan Burke finds himself navigating a perilous landscape when his estranged wife, Reagan, falls victim to the enigmatic Havana Syndrome. This life-altering event ignites a fire within Burke, compelling him to rekindle their relationship while simultaneously embarking on a dangerous mission to uncover the truth behind this debilitating phenomenon.

Higgins masterfully constructs a suspenseful plot that roams from the bustling streets of Washington D.C. to the chilling ambience of Tallinn, Estonia. His characters are richly developed, and the stakes are palpable, drawing the reader into a world where trust is a luxury and danger lurks at every corner. The narrative is heightened by themes of loyalty, sacrifice, and the blurred lines between right and wrong, ultimately leaving readers questioning the true nature of duty.

Higgins draws from his extensive law enforcement background, imbuing the story with authenticity that will resonate with fans of David Baldacci and Michael Connelly. The pacing is relentless, with each chapter ending on a note of suspense that keeps you turning the pages into the night.

The Havana Syndrome is an exhilarating start to a thrilling series, combining deep emotional resonance with the electrifying pulse of espionage. It's a must-read for anyone seeking a blend of heart and heart-stopping action.

Monologues for Kids and Tweens is a thoroughly engaging and practical resource for young performers embarking on their acting journeys. As part of *The Young Actor Series*, this volume stands out for its thoughtful, age-appropriate content that manages to be both entertaining and deeply reflective.

Author Mike Kimmel, a seasoned actor and student of casting legend Michael Shurtleff, has crafted 100 original monologues – a mix of comedy and drama – designed specifically for children and tweens. Each piece is gender-neutral and requires no props or elaborate costumes, making them ideal for auditions, classes, and performance workshops. The monologues explore a wide range of relatable themes, such as responsibility, nostalgia, peer pressure, and grief. Titles like *The Comfy Red Chair and Green Bananas* reflect the everyday situations that are familiar to children but are layered with emotion and subtle life lessons.

What sets this book apart is its clean, family-friendly tone and its commitment to nurturing not just talent, but character. These pieces encourage young actors to connect with real emotions and situations in an accessible, sincere way. As Eva C. Nusbaum points out, these monologues acknowledge the complexity of children's lives, without condescension or sugar-coating.

Educators and parents alike will appreciate the focus on empathy, ethics, and personal growth. This book not only serves as an excellent acting tool, but also as a means of emotional exploration and expression for young people.

An outstanding addition to any young actor's toolkit – both inspiring and skill-building.

NOVEL • STORY • LITERATURE

EDITOR'S CHOICE

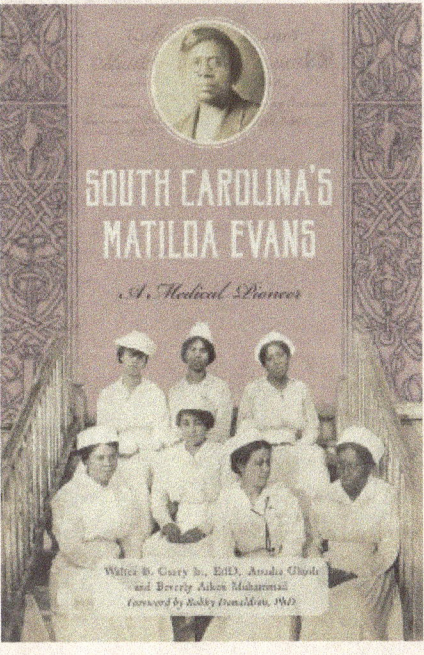

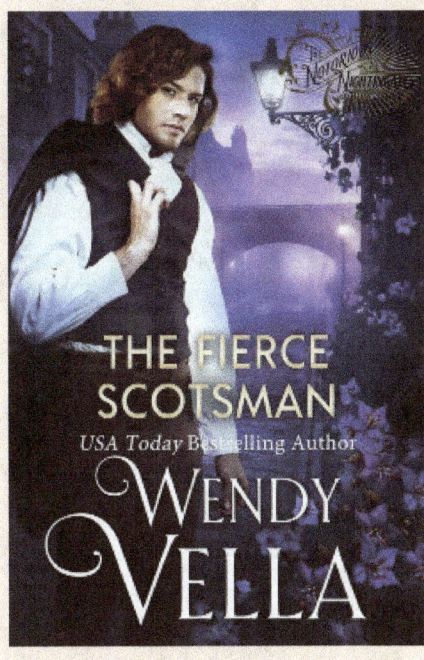

28 VOICES
by Apple An, Georgia Popoff

SOUTH CAROLINA'S MATILDA EVANS
by Dr. Walter B. Curry Jr.

THE FIERCE SCOTSMAN
by Wendy Vella

A powerful and transformative anthology, "28 Voices" celebrates storytelling, offering diverse, authentic narratives that foster deep empathy and connection.

28 Voices is a striking and profoundly moving collection that showcases storytelling at its absolute best. This anthology, edited by Apple An and Georgia Popoff, with a thoughtful foreword by Phil Memmer, unites a diverse array of voices and perspectives, allowing readers to journey through deeply personal yet universally resonant experiences.

The contributors share nonfiction narratives that delve into themes such as identity, resilience, love, and cultural heritage. Each story feels intensely relatable, while also offering fresh insights into lives and experiences that may be worlds apart from your own. Whether it's a heartrending exploration of family bonds, a reflection on cultural roots, or a tale of surmounting challenges, every essay brims with sincerity and depth.

As the top reviews from the United States indicate, 28 Voices has been lauded as "raw and inspiring," with its essays hailed as "essential reading." Readers have remarked on how the anthology fosters empathy and understanding, inviting them to step into the shoes of 28 distinct individuals and forge emotional connections rarely encountered in nonfiction works.

The editorial structuring deserves high praise, with its well-considered pacing ensuring that each voice complements the next. Memmer's foreword is equally impactful, reminding readers of how stories can bridge divides and foster connection across differences.

28 Voices is an extraordinary anthology that celebrates the transformative power of storytelling. A must-read for fans of deeply thoughtful nonfiction, this collection will linger in your mind long after you've turned the final page.

Insightful, inspiring, and deeply practical—Success is a Choice offers a transformative perspective on personal growth and professional success.

In South Carolina's Matilda Evans: A Medical Pioneer, Dr. Walter B. Curry Jr. offers a compelling and richly researched tribute to one of South Carolina's most inspiring yet often overlooked historical figures. Born just four years after the end of slavery, Matilda Arabella Evans rose against the odds to become the first African American woman licensed to practise medicine in the state.

The narrative paints a vivid portrait of a woman who combined extraordinary academic aptitude with unshakeable faith and moral conviction. Evans dedicated her life to advancing healthcare for African Americans, especially children, during the height of segregation—a time when racial inequality permeated every aspect of society. Her efforts weren't confined to the clinic; she was also a civic leader and tireless advocate for education, hygiene, and public health reform.

The collaboration between Curry, Beverly Aiken Muhammad, and Anusha Ghosh adds depth and context, effectively situating Evans's work within the broader historical landscape. The authors seamlessly intertwine personal history with social commentary, creating a narrative that is both educational and profoundly moving.

This book is more than a biography; it is a celebration of resilience, service, and the transformative power of one individual's vision. Dr. Matilda Evans's legacy, as captured in these pages, continues to echo in modern conversations about equity in healthcare and representation in medicine. A must-read for those interested in American history, social justice, and pioneering women.

A thrilling blend of romance and mystery, The Fierce Scotsman captivates with bold characters, emotional depth, and irresistible chemistry.

In The Fierce Scotsman, the final instalment of Wendy Vella's The Notorious Nightingales series, romance and mystery entwine in a richly emotional tale. The narrative follows Mungo Fraser, a brooding Scotsman with a troubled past, and Eliza Downing, a fiercely independent governess who refuses to let society define her.

When Mungo's niece is kidnapped, he is reluctantly reunited with his estranged brother, forcing him to confront familial rifts long buried. The urgency of the situation draws Eliza into the fray, and what begins as a clash of wills between her and Mungo slowly gives way to a simmering and unexpected connection. Their growing bond is deftly portrayed, layered with tension, vulnerability, and an undercurrent of longing that drives the story forward.

Eliza, determined never to fall into genteel obscurity, is an admirable heroine—resilient, sharp-witted, and courageous. Her interactions with Mungo crackle with intensity, providing both emotional depth and romantic charm. As the pair delve into the mystery surrounding the kidnapping, secrets unravel and danger looms, yet it is the emotional revelations between them that truly captivate.

Vella blends historical intrigue with romantic suspense, while also weaving in subtle supernatural undertones that hint at the series' overarching themes. Her prose is elegant and evocative, bringing Regency London—and its darker corners—to vivid life.

A gripping conclusion to a compelling series, The Fierce Scotsman is a tale of redemption, love, and courage. Fans of historical romance with a twist of mystery will find much to savour.

A Journey Through Art, Loss, and Literary Imagination

Michelle Shine blends history, healing, and personal experience to craft powerful narratives that challenge convention and resonate with emotional depth and historical insight.

MICHELLE SHINE
Explores the Unseen Layers of History, Healing and Humanity

Editor's Desk I London

Photo by Caroline True

"Alison, the protagonist, just arrived one day, sitting at her piano where she started to narrate her first person story to me."

Michelle Shine is a literary gem whose works resonate deeply with her readers, blending historical depth, thematic richness, and profound storytelling. With an impressive portfolio that ranges from her longlisted novella The Subtle Art of Healing to her award-winning Song for Ria, Michelle demonstrates an extraordinary ability to weave narratives that both captivate the imagination and stir the soul. Her novel Mesmerised, a compelling intertwining of 19th-century Paris, unorthodox medicine, and impressionist art, showcases her meticulous research and love for history and creativity. Meanwhile, her latest achievement, Ash on the Vine, is an ambitious political and emotional tapestry, spanning continents and generations, cementing Michelle as a bold voice in literary fiction.

Beyond her literary success, Michelle's essays and thought-provoking insights explore the deeper layers of human existence. She carries a unique vision of the world, one that challenges conventions and brings authenticity to both her characters and the pages they inhabit. It is with great privilege that we present our interview with such a talented and visionary author, whose works continue to inspire and leave an enduring mark on the literary landscape.

In your novel "Mesmerised," how did you approach intertwining the lives of historical figures with fictional characters?

Most of the main characters in Mesmerised are historical figures who, as a lover of impressionist art, I had been researching for many years, long before I knew I was going to write about them. As a homeopath, I had also researched Dr Gachet and Dr Jean-Martin Charcot, both of whom worked at La Salpêtrière in Paris. The main theme of the novel is the juxtaposition of unorthodox art and medicine and the lives of the people who practised them in that time and place and so in order to make the plot come alive I had to invent a compelling character who needed healing, alongside the enigmatic Edouard Manet, who also needed healing in real life.

What inspired the narrative of "Song for Ria," and how did you develop its central themes?

I put it out into the ether that I was interested in the 27 club and wanted to write about it. I was working on something else at the time, something dystopian that wasn't going anywhere, and Alison, the protagonist, just arrived one day, sitting at her piano where she started to narrate her first person story to me. I found her fascinating and became merely the conduit for her story throughout the first draft. On reflection, the central themes of child rearing whilst pursuing a career, loss of a loved one and seeking answers via shamanic healing followed by a stay on the Hopi reservation makes Song for Ria semi-autobiographical.

Could you discuss the research process behind your portrayal of 19th-century Paris in "Mesmerised"?

The research for Mesmerised was extensive and as I've already mentioned, took place over many years and started long before I even knew I was going to write the novel. And maybe I never would have, if my soulmate hadn't passed away suddenly one night. I was halfway through an MA in Creative Writing at Birkbeck at the time. I deferred the final year, gave up my homeopathic practice and totally uninspired, hid away from the world for quite a while. When I went back to my writing group, they suggested I start writing about 'that Gachet guy and those artists you love so much'. I took them at their word. My research included: Walking the streets of Paris; Hanging out at the Musée d'Orsay and the Louvre; Reading biographies about the characters. One very important, memorable book is The Private Lives of the Impressionists by Sue Roe. All of these things, together with my own imagination, brought the time and place alive to me in a very vivid way.

How does your background influence the themes and characters in your novels?

Being a homeopath has definitely ignited an interest in what lies beneath the surface. It is a constant motif that seeps into all my storytelling, and leads to a 'thought provoking' theme in all my work.

How has your writing evolved from your earlier works to your latest publications?

My latest novel, Ash on the Vine is, I believe, my most ambitious work to date, taking the reader through flashbacks on two parallel journeys; one from Eastern Europe and the other from Iraq. After WW2, these very different characters meet at Atlit detention camp in what is now called Israel and become man and wife. Present day in the novel is 1989 and the continuing story includes the perspectives of their child and grandchild, and a peace loving woman living in one of the Palestinian territories with her husband and daughter. My research for this novel was extensive. I travelled to Lithuania, Israel, and a Palestinian refugee camp and trawled through many, many historical documents. 1989 was the year of the first intifada and the inception of Hamas, so the story is timely, with the Israeli family becoming a target for a terrorist attack. It is both a family saga and a political thriller. Despite its controversial subject matter Ash on the Vine managed to get itself longlisted for both the Fiction Factory's First Chapter Award and the Yeovil Prize. It has also been chosen as one of Love Reading's indie books they love.

What advice would you offer aspiring authors aiming to craft compelling historical fiction?

Start with an idea that excites you and at least one character you want to get to know and travel alongside. Bring authenticity to the story by doing tons of research, so the time and place you are writing about becomes vivid in your imagination. Create a timeline of important dates and events that you wish to include in your story. Write every day and don't stop until your story is told and you hit the last full stop. Then edit, edit, edit. Oh, and find a writer's circle who will help you by critiquing your work.

> Michelle Shine's writing is rich with empathy, intellectual curiosity and emotional resonance, offering a profound and original perspective in contemporary literary fiction.

Set in 1989 Israel, *Ash on the Vine* follows three generations of Holocaust survivors confronting past traumas amid political unrest. When Sami seeks her grandmother's story, secrets unravel, intersecting lives across cultural divides in a tale of memory, identity, love, and the lasting impact of generational and geopolitical conflict.

Exploring Death, Hope, And Horror Across Realms

Penn Fawn's dark fantasy worlds in Necropolis and The Underworld reimagine the afterlife as a vivid, harrowing continuation where storytelling, philosophy, and visual art converge.

PENN FAWN
CONFRONTS THE AFTERLIFE THROUGH DARK FANTASY AND VISUAL ART

Editor's Desk I London

"What led me to develop it into a series was feedback from a book reviewer who had questions about the background."

Penn Fawn brings readers face-to-face with a shadowy and compelling vision of the afterlife through his dark fantasy series, Necropolis, and its eerie offshoot, The Underworld. Drawing on a rich background in journalism, graphic arts, and digital production, Fawn's career has been interwoven with the printed word in every form. His journey from early fiction experiments stashed away on floppy disks to the publication of acclaimed stories like The Burglar reveals an author who allowed time, experience, and a rekindled creative spirit to shape his voice. What sets Fawn apart is not only the haunting imagination he breathes into his storytelling but the visual dimension he brings through original art, design, and multimedia. With mythic inspiration from sources as disparate as the Bible and Tolkien, his work invites readers to consider the darker terrains of existence, where death does not mean peace, and hope glows dimly in the form of enchanted gems or lone heroes. Through his publishing imprint and artistic ventures, Penn Fawn continues to challenge the borders of genre and media, crafting a uniquely immersive experience in the world of dark fantasy.

What inspired you to create the dark fantasy series, Necropolis, and how did you develop its unique world-building elements?

I wasn't initially thinking about writing a series when I began Necropolis. What led me to develop it into a series was feedback from a book reviewer who had questions about the background and origins of the source material. She mentioned that she hoped I would expand on these elements in future books. I found her points compelling, so I decided to build upon the first book, Necropolis, and that's exactly what I did.

In your spin-off series, The Underworld, you explore a terrifying afterlife. Could you share how you approached blending horror and fantasy in this series?
This might sound like a cliché, but it came very naturally. At no point did blending horror and dark fantasy feel planned, charted, or methodical. The Underworld, as I envisioned it, is a place in the afterlife—a version of hell or purgatory. However, I wanted my Underworld to be more expansive and vividly descriptive than traditional depictions of these realms, such as those in the Bible. While I'm not devout, the Bible—alongside J.R.R. Tolkien's work—was one of my biggest sources of inspiration for this series.

Your short story, "The Burglar," won the Literary Titan Book Award. How did this recognition influence your writing journey?
It didn't influence my journey significantly. Winning awards is great, but the level of prestige determines how much it helps spread the word about your work. While I'm thrilled to have received the Literary Titan Book Award, it's not a widely recognized accolade, so it didn't do much to increase my visibility.

> Fawn masterfully merges horror and fantasy with striking visuals, crafting immersive narratives that explore life beyond death with haunting depth.

As the owner of Darkstar Tees, how do your experiences in graphic arts and clothing design influence the visual aspects of your books?
My background in graphic arts significantly influences the visual elements of my books. Like most authors, I envision the landscapes and creatures in my stories as I write, but sometimes I design these visuals even before finishing the books. If anyone is interested, they can view my artwork on my Pinterest page: Penn Fawn Books.

"Solo" is a short story that delves into the life of a book after its author's death. What inspired you to explore this unique perspective?
The name of the short story is, "The Books," of which Solo is the name of the main character. Although the story is unique—and even comedic—it carries a serious message. It's not just a fun tale about flying books. A bibliophile will likely catch on to its deeper themes quickly. The story is also autobiographical to a degree. I was able to write about the setting in detail because I live in New York, where the story takes place. The Brooklyn Public Library, where Solo finds a home, is a beloved place for me. The story also touches on the tension between traditional and independent publishing.

The Golden Mirage chronicles the journey of men who discover life after death. How do you balance character development with the exploration of philosophical themes in this narrative?
While Lilith, the antagonist, is a central figure, The Golden Mirage also focuses heavily on Hespatia, the "good witch," and her journey. After the many years it took for her to realize her full potential, Hespatia creates the Necropolis within the mountains of Sanctuary, a refuge for men in the Underworld. So, the Necropolis isn't just a burial ground; it's also the name of a magical jewel she crafts to offer hope in the face of seemingly certain or impending doom. The underlying theme is the significance of hope, even in the darkest of times.

Your website mentions a compilation of graphic art meant to introduce readers to your dark fantasy world. How do you see the role of visual art in enhancing the storytelling experience?
Visuals have a more immediate and compelling impact on audiences than the written word. It's no surprise that the film industry reaches broader audiences than books alone. Speaking of visuals, I have a YouTube channel that features music and videos inspired by the settings and characters from Necropolis and The Underworld, including the chief villain, the Necromancer. You can explore them here: Penn Fawn YouTube Channel.

What advice would you offer to aspiring authors looking to blend elements of dark fantasy and horror in their writing?
Study the great works of those who came before you. For me, the Bible is the greatest example of all, but I also recommend devouring everything you can in the genre.

In *Kingdom of the Vampires*, an elderly man named Gib awakens in a strange, eerie realm after death, transformed and bewildered. As he confronts the terrifying reality of a vampire-populated underworld, he questions his beliefs, facing a grim, surreal afterlife in this dark fantasy tale by Penn Fawn.

Blending Mystery, Memory, and Meticulous Research Across Generations

Marshall And Bird Illuminate Untold Histories Through Their Richly Layered Historical Novels

Marshall And Bird craft immersive historical fiction, reviving forgotten voices through detailed research, cultural insight, and dynamic narratives that span centuries—from naval adventures and literacy resistance to Prohibition-era intrigue.

Editor's Desk | London

> Some references are surface, like Pavlov the robo-dog... Other scientific elements are built into the plot."
> – Marshall Highet

> Storytelling is about memory that lives in people, places, and events which, in turn, organise and illuminate the human experience."
> – Bird Jones

Marshall Highet and Bird Jones are two authors whose works captivate readers with their seamless blending of history, imagination, and meticulous research. Together, they craft stories that not only transport us to distant eras but also reflect universal truths that resonate across generations. Marshall Highet, a talented writer and professor, has a body of work as rich as it is diverse, spanning young adult science fiction with *Spare Parts*, swashbuckling historical adventures in *Hold Fast*, and the riveting historical narrative of *Blue-Eyed Slave*. Her ability to construct compelling and ingenious narratives is nothing short of remarkable.

Bird Jones, a professor emerita and seasoned ethnographer, brings a deeply authentic and thoughtful perspective to her storytelling. Her roots in oral history and documentary studies fuel her passion for capturing the voices of the past. From her popular work, *And That's the Way of It: Life in a Maine Village*, to her fascinating collaborations with Highet, Jones's deft ability to illuminate the human experience is unparalleled. Her knack for unearthing overlooked stories and cultural threads infuses her work with richness, insight, and heart.

Together, their collaborations, including *Hold Fast* and the poignant *Blue-Eyed Slave*, carve a unique niche in historical fiction, offering tales that pulse with humanity, complexity, and relevance. Their upcoming novel, *The Washashore*, a masterful blend of coming-of-age drama, mystery, and historical fiction set in 1929 Martha's Vineyard, promises once again to enthral and inspire. Highet and Jones are authors who not only write with precision and passion but also share an infectious curiosity for the intricacies of history. Their thoughtful, collaborative approach to storytelling is a testament to the power of research and imagination united, making history come alive for the modern reader. In the following interview, they share insights about their creative partnership, their inspirations, and the stories behind their distinctive and unforgettable works.

In 'The Washashore', set in the 1920s on Martha's Vineyard, what inspired you to blend mystery, coming-of-age, and historical fiction elements?

MH - It all fell together nicely. I was interested, creatively, in writing a murder mystery because it most resembles an intricate contraption, like a Rube Goldberg machine, in that the plot must be tense and taut until exactly the right moment. As to Martha's Vineyard in the 1920's, what's not to love?

BJ - The Vineyard, an island seven miles off of Massachusetts, was only accessible by boat during 1920's Prohibition. The Vineyard's mariners were some of the best boat handlers in New England, which also made them the best rumrunners. Island life in the twenties by definition was close-knit, affiliative, and diverse. Because of its isolation and the nature of Prohibition, it provides a perfect setting for this story.

'Blue-Eyed Slave' portrays the complexities of 1761 Charles Town. How did you approach depicting the intersection of Jewish and African cultures during this period?

MH - I was astounded at the juxtaposition

of all the different cultures. One of the draws of the South Carolina colony was that it afforded most of its residents' religious freedom and sanctuary from persecution, so many Sephardic Jews came to Charles Town escaping the Inquisition. That in itself blew my mind. People were still running from the Inquisitors in the 18th century? Wow.

BJ - Blue-Eyed Slave is based on two little-known narratives. One is the story of Harry, an enslaved man who ran a literacy school for enslaved children (oddly funded by some of Charles Town's wealthiest citizens) at a time when teaching enslaved people to read and write was against the law. The second story offers a glimpse into the Sephardic community that lived in Charles Town (Charleston's pre-Revolutionary name) because religious freedom was guaranteed in the charter. We used the intersection of these two unconventional perspectives to think about history differently.

'Hold Fast' follows two boys impressed into the British Navy in 1761. What challenges did you face in authentically portraying naval life of that era?

MH - The main challenge for everyone on board was survival; for me, it was language. I had the unenviable task of writing a story, in English, about two native Italian speakers afloat in a sea of English words without a tutor in sight. It was a challenge; italics helped.

Highet and Jones are masterful storytellers whose thought-provoking novels illuminate history with rich detail, depth, and unforgettable characters.

And if you look closely, there is one page, one paragraph, where I flip from Italian to English for good.

BJ - Researching Hold Fast was an athletic as well as an intellectual endeavor. In order to fully understand life at sea, I had to climb the ratlines of a tall ship, scour diaries and primary sources of ship board life, plot accurate courses for navigation, and memorize sail and rig names. It also required a deep dive into naval ships at war, especially at the Battle of Havana. Her Majesty's Navy was a tough life, filled with starvation, lack of sanitation, and endless days at sea.

Marshall, your YA sci-fi novel 'Spare Parts' incorporates educational elements. How do you balance scientific accuracy with engaging storytelling?

MH- Some references are surface, like Pavlov, the robo-dog, who glitches when he hears a bell. Other scientific elements are built into the plot. For example, I used cuttlefish skin's color- and texture-changing capabilities (which are incredible) for the cuttle-camo suits, and my main character is named after my favorite scientist.

Bird, your ethnographic background has taken you from Appalachia to Central Asia. How have these experiences influenced your storytelling approach?

BJ - I was fortunate to do a stint at Duke's Center for Documentary Studies. The best advice I ever got was that my job was to wake the dead and get the living to listen. This is what ethnographers, oral historians, and creative nonfiction writers do.

Storytelling is about memory that lives in people, places, and events which, in turn organize and illuminate the human experience. It is mercurial and interpretative, but the story line, if you listen, stays true to the teller.

Your collaborative writing process involves meticulous research and imaginative storytelling. Can you describe how you integrate these aspects to create compelling narratives?

MH - Seamlessly and effortlessly, always! Kidding. Bird does a lot of heavy lifting in the beginning. She usually finds the spark or thread of the story and starts digging, unearthing primary sources and context. Then we spend time together, her explaining and me asking questions, mapping out the plot. Then I go into writing mode, and feed her each chapter for accuracy checks and consistency. And then—BAM! —it's a book.

BJ - I like to think of history as a giant story full of bonkers characters, impossible events, romance, daring, and surprises at every turn. The joy of writing collaboratively is that I get to pick the starting point and ferret out unsuspecting events and people which Marshall brings alive. It is a total blast.

'The Washashore' is scheduled for publication on June 10, 2025. What themes do you hope readers will connect with in this upcoming novel?

MH - I hope they come for the murder mystery clues and stay for the historical details. It's a marvelous ride through 1929 Martha's Vineyard. Bird has outdone herself finding odd, real details, like Thankful Downs, the MV telephone operator, Dreamland, and the first barn owl sighting on the island.

BJ - I hope readers will find the twenties generally and Prohibition specifically as fascinating as I do. The lives of fishermen turned rumrunners, the poignancy of rural island life, the unintended consequences of political ideas gone astray, and the sheer grit of so many islanders resonate with both Marshall and me, and, I hope, with readers too.

What advice would you offer aspiring authors aiming to write historical fiction that resonates with modern readers?

BJ - Marshall and I use a helpful term: truth pins. If historical fiction is a clothesline, a truth pin is where you hang the story. What are the real facts that make your story more than

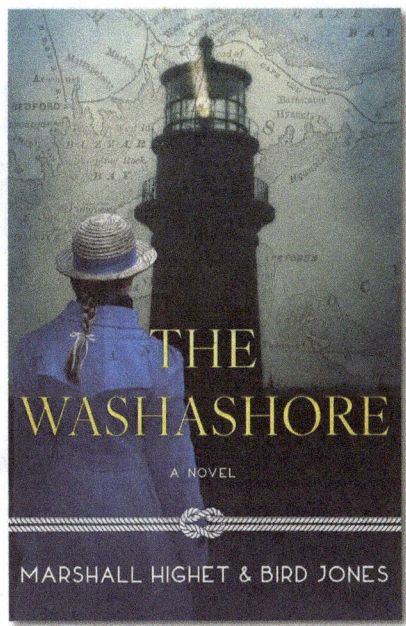

The Washashore by Marshall Highet and Bird Jones is a captivating historical mystery set in 1929 Martha's Vineyard. Combining Prohibition-era intrigue, gangster encounters, and family dynamics, it explores Emily's journey from Midwest outsider to island insider. With rich characters and an atmospheric setting, it delivers suspense and heart in equal measure.

just made-up? Those are your truth pins. And, of course, attention to accuracy and detail is essential.

MH - That the past and its lessons are not so different from what's going on today. A lot of the old clichés are true (although you wouldn't want them in your historical fiction): it is necessary to learn from the past, lest it comes back for a second round.

Reader's House || 47

Navigating Cultures, Identity, and Personal Growth

Michael Shandler discusses his memoir, Karma & Kismet, reflecting on fate, transformation, and leadership. He shares insights on cultural identity, spiritual awakening, and the power of collaboration in personal and professional growth.

MICHAEL SHANDLER
Shares His Extraordinary Journey of Transformation, Leadership, and Spiritual Awakening

Editor's Desk I London

> "These seemingly unrelated events and passages form a whole cloth of karma and kismet… that may hold lessons for others."

Michael Shandler is a storyteller of rare depth, a seeker of wisdom whose journey through continents, cultures, and consciousness has been nothing short of extraordinary. His award-winning memoir, Karma & Kismet — A Spiritual Quest Across Continents, Cultures, and Consciousness, is a masterful reflection on fate, transformation, and self-discovery, shaped by his experiences growing up in apartheid-era South Africa and his lifelong pursuit of spiritual and psychological insight. Kirkus Reviews aptly describes it as "A thoughtful, emotionally forthright, and engaging retrospective."

Beyond his memoir, Shandler's literary contributions span multiple genres, from personal development to leadership and family dynamics. His collaborative works, including The Marriage and Family Book – A Spiritual Guide and The Complete Guide and Cookbook for Raising a Vegetarian Child, showcase his ability to blend practical wisdom with profound human understanding. His writing is not just about sharing knowledge; it is about illuminating pathways for others to navigate the complexities of relationships, identity, and purpose.

In this exclusive interview for Reader's House, Michael Shandler reflects on the forces of karma and kismet that have shaped his life, the lessons he has drawn from navigating diverse cultural landscapes, and his deep commitment to fostering personal and professional growth. His insights are both timeless and timely, offering readers a powerful lens through which to view their own transformative journeys.

What inspired you to write Karma & Kismet, and how did your personal experiences shape the narrative?

I am now an elder pushing eighty. At this stage of life, I've had the good fortune and opportunity as a writer to inventory the key events that shaped my life – from dysfunctional familial relationships that ultimately became transformative, to navigating challenging circumstances, to historical lucky breaks – including war, social and psycho-spiritual-cultural rebellion, to awe-inspiring life and death events, all of which presented unimagined opportunities for change. My story is not that of an important personage, but is perhaps remarkable because these seemingly unrelated events and passages form a whole cloth of karma and kismet – action and destiny – that may hold lessons for others who seek to understand the opportunities for change and soul evolution.

How do you believe the concepts of karma and kismet influence the lives of individuals in the modern world?

Karma and kismet are ancient Eastern and Middle Eastern concepts that speak to the human condition. In that sense, they are timeless principles and have direct application to modern times. Karma can be understood as the actions we take or the circumstances in which we find ourselves, i.e. "Good" karma or "bad" karma. Kismet is fate or destiny, or the unseen hand of a mysterious power that's guides our lives in powerful ways, despite our thoughts and aspirations. We all can point to examples of both of these constructions.

Could you share some of the most transformative moments in your life that helped shape your path to psycho-spiritual wellbeing?

The beginnings of a transformative process occurred when I was dispatched – against my will at age thirteen – to a boarding school where I couldn't speak the language. Later, as a young adult, I lived on a kibbutz in Israel where many of my assumptions about nuclear families were challenged, and where I saw first-hand how collaboration toward desired goals is possible and healthy. My attitude toward war was irrevocably challenged on the battle field of the Golan Heights in Syria in the aftermath of the Six-Day War in 1967. Then when I arrived in North America in 1968, I was introduced to psychedelic drugs and began an introspective journey of awakening that ultimately led me to a spiritual path.

How has your background in leadership and organizational development shaped your approach to life coaching and personal growth?

Over the years, I've worked with hundreds of individuals and teams in large and small organizations and businesses in numerous countries. Leaders create the systems in which individuals and teams operate, and these systems are often based on unexamined values and unquestioned assumptions. Sometimes those systems foster collaboration toward a desired goal, and sometimes those systems (unconsciously) thwart desired outcomes. In the end, it's the people factor that matters. Human beings are capable of examining their value systems, changing their own behavior, and creating conscious systems that harness creativity, collaboration, synergy and foster desired results. All these "working" premises apply to the successful navigation in the journey of life.

In your memoir, you discuss the challenges of navigating multiple cultures. How did those experiences affect your understanding of identity and belonging?

When I was thirteen my world was shaken up and turned inside out by my sudden and unwanted immersion in a culture of tough boys who spoke a language I didn't understand. This immersion lasted for three formative years. These were difficult years, but heralded a journey of discovery about my own cultural and identity assumptions and those of the other boys. We shared some things in common, and sometimes our beliefs were quite different, e.g. our approaches to God, religion and prayer. I began a process of inner seeking – searching for my own core identity – "Who am I?" "What's important to me?" "Where, and with whom do I belong?" This initial awakening from a kind of identity-slumber was pivotal in the long search for belonging that would form the hallmark of my youth and early manhood, and that would ultimately take me into many different cultures on different continents. Later, this search took the form of conscious searching through such disciplines as meditation and self-enquiry, and I learned that many earnest seekers over the generations and centuries had asked similar questions, and that I could benefit from their discoveries.

How do you combine psychological insights with collaborative techniques in your work to foster personal and professional growth?

Psychological insight means something occurred in your experience that you were able to "mine" that ultimately helped you learn, grow, and change. Sometimes this insight comes from listening to the points of view of others who can see aspects or effects of our behavior we may be blind to. This experiential feedback is a fountain of potential wisdom – if we learn to utilize it. In collaborative situations, asking oneself, "How do my assumptions and behavior impact upon those with whom I share a common goal?" "What am I doing that helps cooperation and collaboration, and what gets in the way?" Acting as though I am "response-able" in every situation, I.e. not responsible as in blaming or justifying my actions, but committing to behaviors that are more likely to foster collaboration rather than competition or defensiveness.

What advice would you give to aspiring authors who want to write about their own transformative journeys?

What is the truth of your experience? Why is it worth including? Are there insights that can help others dealing with similar life issues? Do the work until you come to non-blame of others or circumstances, and root out justifications. What lessons did you get? Forget about other peoples' opinions or judgements about what you might say. Accept that some will approve and some likely will not. Is there something universal about your experience from which others might benefit? Find your writing purpose, and let that purpose guide what you focus on and what you leave out. A memoir is not an auto-biography, it's a slice of your life that might have helpful implications for others. If you are not an important person, why would others want to read your book?

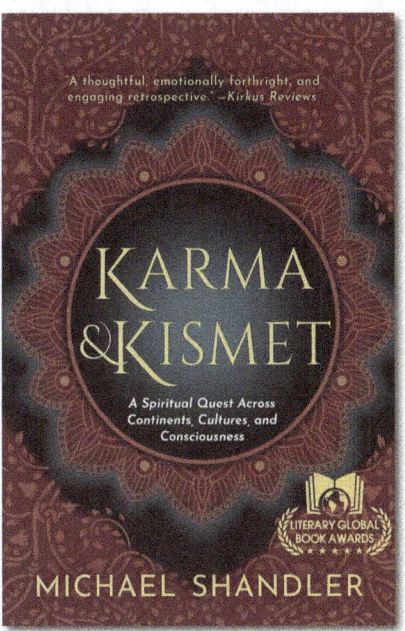

> *A wise and compassionate storyteller, Michael Shandler inspires with profound reflections on identity, spiritual purpose, and conscious, collaborative living.*

Karma and Kismet is a heartfelt memoir tracing Michael Shandler's spiritual journey across cultures and decades. Blending vivid storytelling with deep introspection, it explores fate, identity, and personal growth. Through rich experiences and emotional honesty, the book invites readers to reflect on their own paths toward meaning and belonging.

PROFILE OF EXCELLENCE

EMPOWERING MESSAGES

APPLE AN

ELIZABETH W. ALSOP

Finding Your Own Voice: The Key to Authentic Literary Fiction Writing

Literary fiction has its own rules and norms, very different from academic writing and other intellectual exercises. Mastering these rules and norms is very important. But that is not enough: an author needs to find his or her voice.

I didn't emulate anyone's voice and wouldn't advise any aspiring authors to do the same. I wanted to tell my story inways I felt natural to me. Finding my voice was a process. I knew what I wanted to write about and what emotional and cognitive effects I hoped to generate. But I didn't know if my writing delivered the intended effects. Sharing my drafts with others was tremendously helpful.

Apple An is a professor, author, and advocate for cultural understanding. A professor at Syracuse University since 1995, she has published over 200 academic articles, three books, and received more than 16,500 citations, earning recognition as a leading scholar nationally and internationally. She has received 24 awards for excellence in teaching, research, and service and is the founding editor-in-chief of a major academic journal as well as the inaugural historian for two prominent academic associations.

In 2017, Apple began creative writing at the YMCA's Downtown Writers Center in Syracuse, NY, originally to document her children's Chinese heritage. Inspired by the potential for storytelling to break stereotypes and foster cross-cultural understanding, she began writing short stories, memoirs, and historical novels under the name Apple An. Her 2023 debut memoir, Las Crosses: An Unwavering Journey to a New Life in America, became an Amazon bestseller and award finalist. Her historical novel, Mother of Red Mountains (2024), won accolades from eight award agencies. Apple also created the All-in-One Dotted Journal Notebook and co-edits the Voices Anthology Series. Born during China's Cultural Revolution, she's a mother and guardian of five, a tennis player, ballroom dancer, organic gardener, and avid cultural enthusiast. Learn more at AppleAnBooks.com.

Writing Without Boundaries: Alsop's Advice for Multi-Genre Authors

Elizabeth Winthrop Alsop (www.elizabethwinthropalsop.com) published her first memoir, Daughter of Spies:Wartime Secrets, Family Liesto wide acclaim. She is also the author of over sixty works of fiction under the pen name, Elizabeth Winthrop. Her novels, In My Mother's House (Doubleday)and Island Justice (William Morrow), are both available in e-book editions. Her short story, The Golden Darters, was selected by Robert Stone for Best American Short Stories, has been included in several anthologies of short fiction and was read by the actress Ann Dowd on the nationwide radio program, Selected Shorts. In 2017, she delivered a widely disseminated TED talk entitled, "Risking Exposure: The Creative Life." Some of her over 30 picture book titles include Shoes, Dumpy La Rue, The First Christmas Stocking, Dog Show, The Biggest Parade and Lucy and Henry are Twins.Her books for children have won many awards including the California Young Reader's Medal, the NCTE Notable Book for a Global Society, the New York Times Best Illustrated list, School Library Journal Best of the Best, and the Dorothy Canfield Fisher Award among others. Her essays have been published in Writers Digest, Publishers Weekly among others as well asin collections and anthologies. Her best-selling children's fantasy novels, The Castle in the Attic and The Battle for the Castle,widely considered classics of the genre,have sold over a million copies and are currently under movie consideration.She has recently finished a prequel and is at work on the final book of the series. On Substack, she writes a monthly newsletter, Table of Contents, about publishing and the creative process.

> Stay open to whatever or whomever crosses your path and write it all down, even the bits and pieces that seem inconsequential. They could end up as the core of your next story.

EMPOWERING MESSAGES

PROFILE OF EXCELLENCE

KATE DAMON

RUSSELL PIKE

Crafting Timeless Tales: Margaret Brownley's Advice for Aspiring Authors

Kate Damon (writes as Margaret Brownley) and her husband live in sunny California. When she is not writing, they enjoy spending time with family and friends, raising Monarch butterflies and playing a wicked game of bridge.

Writing as Margaret Brownley, she has published more than forty-six novels and five non-fiction books, including Grieving God's Way, which she wrote following the death of her oldest son. She also wrote for a daytime TV soap.

A New York Times bestselling author, Margaret is known for her memorable characters, impeccable research, and laugh out loud humor. She is also a two-time Romance Writers of America Rita finalist and has won many other writing awards including Readers Choice.

Not counting the book she wrote in sixth grade and the puzzle of the missing socks, Jury Duty is Murder is her first mystery.

> Don't try chasing the market because it's always changing. However, the thing that never changes is the appeal of well-written stories. So familiarize yourself with what readers want in your chosen genre and give it to them..

Fantasy Foundations: Russell Pike's Guide for New Writers in Epic Worlds

> Don't write your magnum opus first. I tried, and it didn't work. Instead, pick an idea you like but aren't in love with, then work it into a novel. Aim for about fifty thousand words. The end result will likely be terrible, but that's fine. Don't expect to paint a masterpiece the first time you pick up a paintbrush.
>
> Once you have a manuscript, invite some critique from your peers, edit it a few times, then put it away. (My first practice novels are buried in the metaphorical desert. The location shall never be revealed.) Start over from the beginning with a new idea and repeat the process. You may be surprised how much more quickly your skills grow when you use this method.

Russell Pike, a child of the eighties, grew up immersed in classics like Ghostbusters, Thunder Cats, and Ninja Turtles (with Michelangelo as the best turtle, in his opinion). At twelve, his mother introduced him to epic fantasy with Robert Jordan's The Eye of the World, sparking a lifelong love of the genre. Since then, he's devoured works by authors such as Anne McCaffrey, Tad Williams, Brandon Sanderson, Jim Butcher, Steven Erikson, Frank Herbert, and David Farland. For Russell, nothing beats the joy of escaping into fantastical worlds and gaining insights about life along the way.

He dabbled in writing during childhood but took his craft seriously later in college, initially aiming to make money for grad school applications. However, he quickly realized that becoming a novelist is no shortcut to quick cash. The defining moment came when he chose editing chapters over watching a forgettable movie with his family, recognizing that writing had become his passion.

Over the next decade, Russell committed to honing his craft, sacrificing TV, movies, and sleep to write. Along the way, he had the honor of collaborating with industry legends like David Farland and received unwavering support from his family. Beyond writing, Russell enjoys camping hikes (especially hammock-friendly ones), volunteering as a sled dog handler, and indulging his love for fast cars and remote mountain roads. His journey has been one of persistence and discovery, fueled by his devotion to storytelling and adventure.

PROFILE OF EXCELLENCE

DANIEL HAYES

Subversive Narratives: The Art of Storytelling Beyond Moral Lessons

Daniel Hayes lives on the family farm where he grew up in Upstate New York, at the southern end of scenic Washington County. Born April 17th, 1952, he attended school in Greenwich, New York, which became the fictional village of Wakefield in his novels. Having retired from many years of teaching English at Troy High School and Creative Writing at Hudson Valley Community College, he now spends his time traveling, creating videos for his Adventures with Hayeski YouTube channel, and philosophizing about life. His goal, in addition to writing more books (a fifth, My Kind of Crazy, is nearly ready to go!), is to someday see film or TV versions of his novels. Having fielded a number of queries from various producers over the years, he hopes, eventually, to be able to put Tyler and Lymie and the rest of his cast of characters up on the big screen. (He'd even settle for the small screen!) Should this happen, due to his considerable acting skills, he feels he should, at the very least, be considered for the role of the dead body in The Trouble with Lemons. He's already perfecting his ability to float face down for extended periods.

Having sat through way too many earnest and well-intentioned graduation speakers, often students themselves dispensing life lessons to their fellow graduates, and being aware that my own life is still very much a work in progress, I try to reign myself in when I feel the need to pontificate on any subject, all too often with limited success. So with abject apologies, here I go again: Writers (especially those who write for the young) must resist the temptation to make their stories teaching tools. A good story will present dilemmas and choices which often reflect the writer's worldview, but using stories to present "lessons" in life from one who is older and feels wiser can greatly reduce their power. Mark Twain, one of my all-time favorite writers, spoofed this moralizing directly in "Story of the Bad Little Boy," featuring a main character who did everything "wrong" and, against all the unspoken dictates of children's literature of that era, happily received the benefits of his wrongdoing, getting away scotfree and fulfilled. Twain played with this theme a little more indirectly in The Adventures of Huckleberry Finn, whose titular character rose above contemporary morals, choosing instead to rely on his own moral compass. This heresy resulted in Huck Finn being, not merely criticised, but outright banned from many schools and libraries. The best stories, I feel, are always at least a little subversive to the status quo, and without authors being willing to challenge the accepted beliefs of the day, society might be a lot less likely to evolve.

EMPOWERING MESSAGES

CYNTHIA WOOLF

Navigating Writer's Block: Strategies from Best-Selling Author

Cynthia Woolf is an accomplished author recognized for her prolific output of 86 novels, which encompass a diverse array of genres. Her body of work includes 66 historical western romances, 11 contemporary romances, 2 contemporary romance novellas, 1 historical western romance novella, and 6 sci-fi space opera romances—genres she affectionately dubs "westerns in space." In addition, she has published 12 boxed sets and two short stories, demonstrating her versatility and commitment to storytelling.

Cynthia's passion for writing was evident from an early age; she wrote her first story at just ten years old, inspired by a childhood crush. The seed for her debut novel, *Tame A Wild Heart*, was planted through a tale her mother shared about meeting her father on a ranch in Creede, Colorado. Although the novel diverges from this true story, it reflects her connection to the landscapes and narratives of her upbringing.

First, every writer I've talked to faces writers block at one time or another. It doesn't matter if you do a lot of plotting or none. Writer's block can happen to anyone. When I get it, I reread what I've already written and usually that will send me on the path I need to follow. Sometimes I have to get away from that project and start another before the answer to the to what is blocking me reveals itself. There are times that neither of those work and I just have to wait for the characters to talk to me and tell me where to send the story. I know that sounds odd, but you'll find that most authors will refer to their characters talking to them. In my experience, talking to other authors of various genres, it's just what happens when you are a writer, regardless of what you write. It's the characters that guide the story, after all.

Born in Denver and raised in the mountains near Golden, Cynthia enjoyed a spirited childhood filled with adventure and friendship. Her formal writing journey began in 1990 with a round-robin story project with coworkers, which led her to the Colorado Romance Writers conference. There, a chance encounter with author Catherine Coulter inspired her to pursue her writing goals seriously.

After facing rejections, including one from Avon, Cynthia's determination shone through when she was laid off in 2011. Utilizing her unemployment period to refine her work, she published her first three novels, marking the start of her successful career. Cynthia attributes much of her success to the unwavering support of her husband, Jim, and the encouragement from her critique partners, which has allowed her creativity to flourish in the ever-evolving world of romance literature.

EMPOWERING MESSAGES   PROFILE OF EXCELLENCE

KATHERINE E. HAMILTON

SAWYER BENNETT

Katharine E. Hamilton: Crafting Stories and Guiding Dreams in the World of Publishing

Sawyer Bennett: A Legal Mind Turned Literary Star—Insights on Building a Lasting Romance Author Career

Katharine has been writing since 2008. She's written over 40 titles and has helped multiple authors discover their publishing dreams through private publishing consulting. She's sold over 500,000 books, won multiple reader's choice awards, and achieved best seller status on 36 titles. She continues writing heartwarming stories today.

For aspiring authors I would say, don't give up. Keep going. Keep writing. Get the first draft FINISHED. You cannot edit a blank page. It will not be perfect. And hey, no one expects it to be perfect, that's what editing is for! Just get the words down and get your story out, everything else will start falling into place after it. Just get the words down and take it one step at a time.

She is a graduate of Texas A&M University, a wife, mom, teacher, consultant, and entrepreneur. She loves traveling to Ireland for fun and inspiration, but she calls the Texas coast home, alongside her husband, two sons and their dog named Paws.

I've been self-publishing since 2013, which was right at the start of the big indie author boom. Timing certainly played a role in my journey, and the landscape has become far more competitive, making it even more crucial for aspiring authors to approach this as a serious business, not just a hobby. If you want a lasting career in romance writing, you have to be all in—treating it like a full-time job with the dedication and consistency that any successful career demands.

One of the best things you can do is immerse yourself in the author community. There are so many fantastic groups filled with invaluable advice, resources, and support. Learning from others and staying adaptable in an ever-changing industry is key.

But above all—write, write, write. You can't build a career on just one book. Longevity comes from continually producing quality stories, growing your backlist, and treating this like a marathon, not a sprint. Success in this industry isn't just about talent; it's about persistence, discipline, and the willingness to keep showing up for your readers.

New York Times, USA Today, and Wall Street Journal Bestselling author Sawyer Bennett uses real life experience to create relatable stories that appeal to a wide array of readers. From contemporary romance, fantasy romance, and both women's and general fiction, Sawyer writes something for just about everyone.

A former trial lawyer from North Carolina, when she is not bringing fiction to life, Sawyer is a chauffeur, stylist, chef, maid, and personal assistant to her very adorable daughter, as well as full-time servant to her wonderfully naughty dogs.

Blending Horror And Maritime Adventure

RYAN BERRIDGE

Weaves Horror and Adventure into Gritty Tales of Pirates and Monsters

BY DAN PETERS | LONDON

Ryan Berridge is a name rapidly gaining traction among fans of horror and adventure fiction, and deservedly so. Hailing from Sheffield, England, Ryan has carved out a unique niche by blending the unnerving terror of supernatural horror with the gritty realism of survival and leadership tales. A self-published tour de force whose works consistently earn high praise, his ability to juggle complex narratives while making each twist and turn deeply human is nothing short of remarkable.

From the thrilling ambiguity of his debut collection *Where Were You? Ten Terrifying Tales*—a compilation of chilling pandemic-era short stories—to the sweeping brutality and moral dilemmas of his pirate-themed *Rattler Trilogy*, Ryan has demonstrated a profound ability to craft stories that are both visceral and thought-provoking. The trilogy, comprising *The Rattler*, *Snake Huntress*, and *The Golden King*, has cemented his reputation as a writer unafraid to explore the darkest recesses of human experience and ambition, all while pushing the boundaries of genre fiction.

What stands out most about Ryan is not simply the narrative depth of his novels but the personal and emotional truths underpinning his work. Twelve-hour workdays, sleepless nights, and the challenges of parenting have forged a writer who channels raw emotion into his characters and stories. His ability to merge historical adventure with the murky tension of horror—a skill inspired by literary titans such as Stephen King and Bernard Cornwell—is nothing short of enchanting.

As you dive into this interview, prepare to explore the mind of an author who refuses to flinch from the messy complexity of human choices, the moral grey areas we all navigate, and the frightening unknowns lurking just below the surface—all while keeping you gripped with startlingly vivid action scenes. If you're new to Ryan Berridge, I suspect you'll come away wondering why you hadn't discovered his bold and compelling work sooner.

Your "Rattler Trilogy" centres on a young pirate, Sam – how did your background growing up in Sheffield influence the gritty, survivalist portrayal of his journey?

The anger came much later for me. My childhood was perfectly normal, but as I entered my thirties my wife became pregnant as I started the Rattler book. My daughter was then born prematurely and we spent a total of six weeks in the hospital. During that time the company I worked for were less than supportive with no sensitivity to the situation. It left me angry and bitter for a long time and a lot of that came out in the first book, with the other two written under a similar cloud.

Karen King shares insights into her transition across genres, her writing process, influences, and themes while unveiling the joys and challenges behind her latest psychological thriller Don't Trust Him.

In The Rattler, mythical creatures appear at sea – what inspired you to blend maritime adventure with supernatural horror?

This is an interesting question. Whilst there are mentions of mythical creatures in the book, the descriptions themselves can be explained in our everyday world. This was deliberately ambiguous on my part, similar to the tales sailors have been telling for as long as they have been on sea. It is up to the reader to decide whether the monsters are real or exaggerated.

Snake Huntress sees Sam become a pirate captain – how did you deepen his moral complexity and leadership arc in book two?

The reader follows Sam's journey from the very first steps aboard the ship to the highest position. He was thrust into decisions where he had to choose the lesser of two evils, sometimes he chose wrong but that is only natural. He leaned on the advise of the senior ranks but still made his own decisions for better or worse.

The Golden King concluded the trilogy in July 2023 – what thematic resolution did you aim to achieve with Sam's final confrontation?

I needed Sam to experience the absolute peak of his abilities and then to see him begin to fall from his perch. I wanted readers to be completely unsure of where the story was heading in the final ten pages.

Your debut Where Were You? Ten Terrifying Tales is pandemic themed horror – how did writing pandemic short stories prepare you for large scale adventure narratives?

Being new to writing I wanted to explore different environments, characters and styles. Some of the stories are third person, some first, some are induvial characters, some have multiple. One story has two narratives running simultaneously. The idea was to find my style and it really helped to show what worked and what didn't when revisiting the stories for further revisions.

Reviews praise the intense, visceral action in The Rattler – can you describe your process for choreographing brutal scenes without alienating readers?

I made a conscious decision that I would only do one draft of these scenes. I wanted to capture the chaotic and unpredictable nature of the battle. There was no planning, just me putting words on the page whilst imagining myself in the heat of what was happening. It needed to be real and I didn't want anything to be gruesome for gruesome's sake. There is one particular scene in the Rattler (and I'm sure

54 || Reader's House

Ryan Berridge's *The Golden King* delivers a stunning conclusion to the *Rattler Trilogy*, weaving dark, maritime adventure with emotional depth. Packed with gripping action, moral complexity, and unpredictable twists, Berridge masterfully captures readers' imaginations while exploring the tumult of leadership and legacy. A must-read for fans of pirate lore and unflinching storytelling.

any reader will know which one I mean) where the other characters gave the description of what was happening, I felt it wasn't necessary for me to go into the detail, that would have pushed the book into a completely different category.

You cite Stephen King and Bernard Cornwell as influences – how do you balance King's horror tension with Cornwell's historical adventure style in your pirate series?

Pirates have long been romanticised in the entertainment space, from Pirates of the Carribean to children's books, whereas in reality they were not nice people. I therefore felt it was important to flavour the story with a little darkness, with readers not quite knowing where the story was going or whether the monsters were real. At the start of the trilogy I was in the midst of the reading the Last Kingdom series and it just clicked, that was exactly the style I wanted. You therefore have a protagonist who doesn't know anything about the world he has been thrust into, and the readers who have to follow him on the journey and work out for themselves whether the monsters are real.

What single piece of advice would you offer aspiring authors looking to blend genre elements as distinctly as you have in horror adventure fiction?

Write. That's it. Just keep writing and re-drafting. For each book in the trilogy I wrote 1,000 words a day. Some days they were complete nonsense and required an entire re-write, some days the words came so naturally I lost myself (this was often where the best work was done). The important thing for me was to just keep being consistent, that way I found that the book was never far from my mind and the story was probably written in my subconscious.

Ryan Berridge, acclaimed author of The Rattler Trilogy and Where Were You?, blends horror and adventure with heart.

> *I wanted to capture the chaotic and unpredictable nature of the battle."*

Ryan Berridge

Exploring Her Journey, Creative Process, And Advice For Aspiring Writers

SY MONTGOMERY

Her Journey Into The Minds And Hearts Of The Animal Kingdom

BY DAN PETERS | LONDON

Sy Montgomery's life reads like an epic adventure, woven with threads of scientific curiosity, poetic insight, and fearless exploration. A veritable force of nature herself, Montgomery has immersed her life in the beauty, complexity, and astonishing intelligence of the world's creatures, from tarantulas in French Guiana to octopuses in the Pacific Ocean. Whether swimming with piranhas in the Amazon or befriending snapping turtles in freshwater streams, Montgomery brings an unparalleled depth of connection to every project she undertakes.

Her works—masterpieces like *The Soul of an Octopus*, a finalist for the National Book Awards, and *The Good Good Pig*, her memoir of life with an extraordinary pig named Christopher Hogwood—are not mere books but transformative experiences. They are beacons of understanding, offering readers profound insights into the lives of animals and our shared thread within the tapestry of existence. With 38 books under her belt, ranging from children's literature honoured by awards like the Cook Prize, to National Geographic documentaries highlighting man-eating tigers and rehabilitated bear cubs, Montgomery has shaped the narrative of human-animal connections like no other writer of our time.

Lauded by *The New York Times* as "equal parts poet and scientist" and by *The Boston Globe* as "part Indiana Jones and part Emily Dickinson," Montgomery is not simply a chronicler of nature's marvels but its true advocate. Her work resonates deeply in this critical moment of human history, where, as she herself puts it, we stand "on the cusp of either destroying this sweet, green Earth—or revolutionising the way we understand the rest of animate creation."

In this enriching interview, Montgomery invites us into the world of chickens with *What the Chicken Knows*, the tender resilience of injured turtles in *Of Time and Turtles*, and the intricate minds of cephalopods in *Secrets of the Octopus*. Blending scientific observation with intimate personal engagement, her narratives are alive with wisdom, humility, and a sense of wonder that reminds us of the intricate bonds tying us together and the lessons we must learn from the creatures who share our planet. Whether writing for adults, children, or a universal audience, Montgomery's voice transcends barriers and connects us all. It is no surprise she has captivated hearts across platforms, featured on TEDx stages, award-winning podcasts, and as a literary contributor to the most esteemed publications.

Sy Montgomery's life work is a testament to the extraordinary gifts nature offers and the wisdom awaiting those who listen. This dialogue is not just an interview—it's an invitation to fall in love with the world afresh through her eyes. Prepare to be inspired to embrace the "sweet, green, living world" in all its luminous glory.

In What the Chicken Knows, how did your personal experiences with chickens reshape your understanding of these often-overlooked birds?

I always start my adventures with animals with "Beginner's Mind." I knew, of course, that some people dismiss the intelligence of birds, and particularly chickens, as "bird brains." But I also knew from my life getting to know creatures from tarantulas to tapirs and from pink dolphins to pigs that humans typically underestimate the powers of those unlike ourselves. I was not surprised to find chickens are smart. But I was delighted to discover that in many ways, their smarts as so like our own. They can recognize and remember 100 different faces, including human faces. Their special mapping abilities are superb. And the pecking order is far more about order than pecking, because relationships are extremely important to chickens. They want to belong in their community or group, just like we do. They are capable of reasoning, remembering, and communicating complex information—such as whether a predator is coming quickly or slowly, from sky or land. Yet, at the same time, their instincts are sharp, and sometimes direct them to behave in ways we find baffling. At the sight of blood, for instance, chickens will attack even their closest kin. Nobody knows why they do this.

Award-winning author Sy Montgomery delves into the intelligence, resilience, and emotional connections of animals, showcasing how her adventures inspire a deeper understanding of life shared with fellow creatures.

Secrets of the Octopus builds upon your earlier work; what new insights into octopus intelligence and behaviour did you uncover during this project?

So much new science has been done since Soul of an Octopus was published in 2015! One of the most exciting discoveries at least partially answers one of the questions that burned in me the whole time I was working with my octopus friends at New England Aquarium starting in 2011: why did these animals, who are famously solitary, even want to interact with me at all? As it turns out, many species of octopuses are not solitary after all. Even the Giant Pacific octopus can often be found in aggregations in the wild. Other species inhabit octopus "cities" like Octopolis in Australia, where more than a dozen individual Octopus tetricus might den in an area only 2-3 meters in diameter. Other species seem to cohabit with favored mates. And yet more may develop partnerships with other species for the purpose of hunting together!

Your memoir How to Be a Good Creature intertwines personal stories with animal encounters; how have these relationships influenced your perspective on human-animal connections?

That book tells the stories of how 13 animals taught me so many of the most important skills of my life: how to find what you want to do with life. How to find the path to lead you there. How to forgive someone who has hurt you. How to make a family. (Hint: it's not about genes or blood; it's about love and not confined to just one species!) My relationships with animals have shown me that animals are, just as native peoples around the world have known for eons, great teachers. If we fail to pay attention to these other creatures around us, and concentrate our attention of humans alone, our lives will be as impoverished as if we only listened to one kind of music, ate one kind of food, and never left our own room.

In Of Time and Turtles, what lessons did you learn about resilience and healing from working with injured turtles?

Turtles survived the asteroid impact that killed off the dinosaurs. They survived the Ice Ages. Each turtle who lives to adulthood has survived a

56 || Reader's House

Sy Montgomery holds a copy of *National Geographic*, featuring a stunning octopus cover that highlights her passion for the natural world and marine life exploration.

gamut of predators, from racoons, dogs and skunks who dig up their eggs to crows and herons and chipmunks, who eat the hatchlings. And a turtle may well survive an injury that would surely kill another creature. Turtles teach you to have faith. Turtles teach you to cultivate patience. And helping turtles—literally repairing broken shells—showed me the renewing power of taking a hand in healing our broken world.

The Soul of an Octopus explores consciousness in cephalopods; what challenges did you face in conveying their inner lives to readers?

The challenge one faces is the notion, pervasive in Western culture, that only humans have thoughts, feelings, memories, and knowledge. Which is of course absurd if you accept the evidence for evolution: being able to think and feel, to learn from experience and plan for the future, has obvious adaptive value for many organisms, not just our kind. So I followed the advice that guides every good journalist: show, don't tell. I wrote about my octopus friends' behavior—and generally let readers draw their own conclusions.

Your adventures often involve close interactions with wildlife; how do you balance scientific observation with personal engagement in your narratives?

The narrative provides a scaffolding for the science. Of course the science is interesting on its own—that some turtles communicate with one another while still in the egg, that many species learn mazes as fast as lab rats, that some sea turtles shells glow in the dark. But it means so much more when it applies to a specific individual who you have come to know over the narrative journey of the book.

Having written for both adults and children, how do you adapt your storytelling approach to suit different audiences while maintaining authenticity?

Many of my books written for younger audiences—including those I wrote for the Scientists in the Field series I founded with photographer Nic Bishop—are reviewed as if they were written for adults. Kids are smart. Because they haven't been alive as long as adults, their vocabularies are smaller, and their knowledge about the world less extensive. But other than this I think we're largely the same. I use shorter and fewer words in my books for kids. But I respect their smarts and honor their curiosity just as I would a smart adult's. One of the smartest and most experienced people I know is the Emmy award winning actor and podcaster Alan Alda. He's been alive for nearly 9 decades. He's had his own science TV show. Do you want to know his most pressing question when I introduced him to New England Aquarium's resident Giant Pacific Octopus?

"Where does its poop come out?" (Answer: from the siphon it uses to jet through the sea.) I think most adults are in fact interested in knowing such things but aren't brave enough to ask out loud!

What advice would you offer to aspiring authors aiming to write compelling narratives about the natural world?

Go out and live in the real world—the sweet, green, living world—be it in your backyard or in some exotic location. Just pay attention. What does it smell like, feel like, sound like to be in this place at this time with these creatures? How do they make you feel? And when you write, think of writing to a dear friend, knowing that every vivid detail you bring back from your experience to share is a gift to them, and a love song to this splendid, fragile, incandescent life.

> *"Our lives will be impoverished if we only listen to one kind of music, eat one kind of food, and never leave our room."*
>
> # Sy Montgomery

Inspired By Family, Fantasy, And Magic
NATALIA MORRIS
Sheds Light On Her Creative Journey Through Storytelling And Illustration

BY BEN ALAN | LONDON

Natalia Morris commands attention not only as an author but also as a captivating illustrator whose works brim with imagination, charm, and heartfelt resonance. Her distinct ability to weave whimsical narratives with evocative artistry has earned her a cherished place in the world of children's literature. With her debut creation *Quest for Cookies*, Natalia delivers a tale that is both enchanting and culturally enriching, captivating the hearts of readers young and old. Gnomey's delightful journey, threaded with lavender-dipped nostalgia and universal themes of familial love, exemplifies the gift Natalia bestows upon her audience—a perfect blend of curiosity, kindness, and a sprinkling of magic.

From storytelling that reflects the tenderness of relationships to illustrations bursting with vibrancy, Natalia's works are a triumph of creativity and meaning. Notably, her talent extends to her illustration of *You Are Not Your Meltdown* by Desirea Binning, showcasing her versatility as an artist of boundless potential. Triumphing with the #1 spot in multicultural children's literature charts, *Quest for Cookies*' impact on young minds is undeniable, promising enduring success in libraries and beyond.

It is rare to encounter a creator who balances their narrative voice with harmonious visual rhythm so seamlessly, all while embracing baking traditions and translating life's tender moments into relatable tales and intricate artwork. As we delve into her journey, Natalia's reflections on persistence and authenticity not only inspire but illuminate how her work emanates the joy and depth she holds dear. In this issue, join us as we explore the thoughtful world of Natalia Morris—a truly radiant force in contemporary children's literature.

In Quest for Cookies, what inspired Gnomey's love for lavender cookies, and how did you weave multicultural elements into the narrative?

Gnomey's love of lavender cookies comes straight from a special place in my heart. My grandmother makes these delicious cookies for me anytime I go over to visit. I tried to infuse a lot of myself into both the story and the Gnomey character. I believe that stories based partly in the real world are more impactful for readers.

As for the multicultural aspect, the book's heart has a universal message:

grandparents are awesome and deserve our time and attention. Too often, life gets busy and those grandparent-grandchild relationships fade. But across cultures, there's deep value in honoring our elders. I wanted to reflect that in a way that speaks to kids everywhere.

Your illustrations are richly detailed—what techniques or media did you use to bring Gnomey's world to life?

The entire book was illustrated on my iPad using a platform called Procreate. I drew inspiration from a Domestika course taught by children's book author and illustrator, Ramona Wultschner. I also applied a technique I learned while earning my Fine Art Diploma. This technique is simply "do not completely render something and then move on, work on the piece as a whole". As an example, if drawing a portrait, one should not completely render the eyes before working on the rest of the face because the eyes will feel out of place. I carried that approach through the entire book. It's a small detail, but it helps the illustrations feel cohesive and alive.

The book hit #1 in the multicultural children's charts—how did that success shape your creative path?

That milestone was huge. Not only did it affirm my storytelling, but it opened doors. I was invited to illustrate You Are Not Your Meltdown by Desirea Binning, which required a completely different artistic style. That challenge was incredibly rewarding and made me realize I wanted to pursue illustration more seriously. Since then, I've revamped my website, expanded my portfolio, and started marketing myself as a professional children's book illustrator.

You recently celebrated the book arriving in libraries—with eight holds! How did that feel?

Honestly? Like a warm hug from the universe. Having your work out there is one thing, but knowing people are actively waiting to read it is incredibly affirming. It made me feel like I'm on the right path—and gave me the confidence to keep exploring this creative avenue.

Baking features heavily in your social media—does it influence your storytelling or illustration process?

Absolutely! Baking is deeply woven into this book. Three of the recipes in Quest for Cookies are straight from my own kitchen. The lavender cookies are my grandmother's, the raspberry muffins come from a generational recipe I now make with my daughter and husband, and Bean's carrot cake is a party favorite. While future stories may branch into other themes, for this book, baking was one of the focal points.

As both author and illustrator, how do you balance narrative pacing with visual rhythm?

I always imagined reading the story aloud to my daughter (I was pregnant with her when I wrote and published the book). It has to sound the way I want it to feel—playful, silly, heartfelt. Interestingly, I actually illustrate first. The words come later and are molded to match the energy and rhythm of the artwork. It's an unusual approach, but for me, it ensures the visuals and text dance together on the page.

Natalia Morris shares her artistic journey, illustrating and writing heartfelt tales like Quest for Cookies, and discusses multicultural themes, baking inspirations, visual techniques, and advice for aspiring creators.

Quest for Cookies by Natalia Morris is a charming and heartwarming tale that blends humour, life lessons, and delicious nostalgia. With whimsical illustrations and a lovable protagonist, Gnomey, this enchanting adventure celebrates kindness, courage, and the wisdom of grandparents. A delightful read packed with sweetness and memorable moments for young readers!

#1 RANKING IN MULTICULTURAL CHILDREN'S CHARTS

What was the most challenging scene to create in Quest for Cookies, and how did you push through it?

Definitely the spooky mushroom forest. I had a vivid image in my head, but translating that to paper was tricky. It required several "mushroom studies" before I got it right. I just kept sketching until it matched the vision. That page taught me that persistence really pays off—and that fungi are harder to draw than you think.

What advice would you give to aspiring children's authors and illustrators?

My advice would be to only make something if you really believe in your product. I think that applies to a lot of things outside of the literary world also. If you are producing something that does not come from your heart, it will show. In this case, readers will not be as invested in what you have to say. Your illustrations won't be as captivating. Create something because you have a vision and love what you do. Love your work and others will too.

> *Stories based partly in the real world are more impactful for readers."*

Natalia Morris

Natalia Morris, Author And Illustrator Of Quest For Cookies, Inspires With Her Creativity, Passion For Baking, And Vibrant Artistry.

Unveiling Emotional Truths In Fiction
J. D. EDWARDS
Takes Readers On Thrilling Journeys Through Fantasy History, And Mythology

BY BEN ALAN | LONDON

J. D. Edwards stands as a beacon of creative brilliance in the world of literature, crafting stories that traverse the realms of Epic Fantasy, Historical Fiction, Horror, Theology, and Poetry with unparalleled mastery. A gifted storyteller with a theologian's depth, Edwards possesses the rare ability to breathe life into ancient legends while weaving intensely human narratives of hope, grief, and redemption. His works offer readers not just an escape but a transformative experience, leaving one to linger in introspection long after the final page has been turned.

With accolades from prestigious organisations such as The Charl Ormond Williams Foundation, Carolina Bards, and TCK Publishing, Edwards has carved out an indelible space for himself in both historical research and speculative fiction. His historical novel *Indomitable: The Story of Eliza Harris*, an Amazon Top 10 Bestseller, exemplifies his painstaking attention to detail, marrying historical fact with the emotional resonance of personal struggle. Meanwhile, his epic fantasy series, *The Faerie Chronicles*, immerses readers in a richly constructed world, where Celtic myth meets modern landscapes, and every name and place brims with meaning.

Edwards' ability to straddle narrative genres showcases his extraordinary versatility and boundless creative energy, whether he's illuminating the dark corners of history or building fantastical worlds steeped in biblical prophecy and Celtic lore. His latest release, *The Scions of Faerie*, sets the foundation for yet another sweeping, multi-layered saga—one that invites readers to journey into lands where the boundaries blur between myth and reality, geography and imagination.

In this exclusive interview, J. D. Edwards opens up about his creative drive, his commitment to emotional authenticity, and the meticulous research process that both enriches his historical novels and breathes life into his fantastical realms. Whether delving into grief, identity, or the cost of magic, Edwards' characters embody journeys that unerringly reflect the truths of human experience. As readers of *The Faerie Chronicles* and *Indomitable* will attest, every story from his pen is a testament to the transformative power of words—and to the enduring legacy of a masterful storyteller at work.

In The Scions of Faerie, Ian's journey intertwines Celtic mythology with modern settings – what inspired that fusion, and how did you research the ancient lore?

In 2003, my wife and I discovered we were expecting again, after the heartbreaking loss of our first son, Jonathan Ian Edwards. That moment marked the genesis of The Faerie Chronicles. I set out to write an epic fantasy that would blur the line between fiction and reality—where myths breathe, allegory hides in plain sight, and every shadow hints at a deeper truth.

I knew I wanted to breathe new life into ancient legends. I wasn't interested in imitation or trope. I wanted to blur the lines between fantasy and reality so seamlessly that readers would begin to question where one ended and the other began.

To avoid mirroring contemporary interpretations, I turned to texts from the 18th and 19th centuries. These sources felt raw, elemental, and closer to the original telling. That decision allowed me to rediscover Celtic mythology with

J. D. Edwards discusses his fantasy and historical works, emotional arcs, rigorous research methods, and multi-genre storytelling, offering insights into creativity, authenticity, and the transformative power of literature.

fresh eyes and weave it into the present day without compromising its mystery.

The Soul Stones of Faerie deepens your faerie world; how did you decide which mythical elements to expand or reinterpret?

In the foreword to The Lord of the Rings, J. R. R. Tolkien writes, "The story grew in the telling." That line resonated within my soul. When I wrote The Soul Stones of Faerie, I compiled a loose collection of plot points and mythical elements in Microsoft OneNote. I didn't treat them as a strict roadmap, but rather as inspiration that could evolve as the story unfolded.

I never knew how the story would end until I reached the final page, and I used the same strategy for the other books in the series. This freedom allowed the narrative to take on a life of its own—one in which I could lose myself completely. It's that same sense of wonder and discovery that draws readers into Faerie, helps them connect with the characters, and allows the magic to take root within their hearts.

Your Faerie Chronicles shift in tone across the series; how did you balance YA adventure with deeper themes like loss and identity?

You cannot have light without shadow. As the series progresses, it embraces more adult themes—loss, death, and betrayal—but I counterbalance those with moments of love, redemption, and cheeky humor. The Faerie Chronicles is a coming-of-age epic that invites readers of all ages to confront hard questions at their own pace and in their own way.

Much like Star Trek, these books explore difficult social and emotional terrain through the lens of an imagined world. That distance gives readers room to wrestle with reality while never losing the thrill of wonder, magic, and possibility.

With Indomitable, you moved into historical fiction—how did your genealogical writing influence your portrayal of real-life characters?

I began researching my ancestry in 1989, and in 2012, while tracing my family's ties to the Underground Railroad, I stumbled upon a manuscript interviewing my distant cousin, Reverend John Rankin. In it, he recounted his role in helping a young runaway slave named Eliza Harris; an account that would shape everything to follow. That discovery pulled me deep into the rabbit hole. I spent the next decade hunting for any shred of evidence that might reveal the path Eliza traveled, the stations she stopped at, and the people who risked everything to help her.

Indomitable emerged from that journey. The only fiction in the novel lies in how I connect Fact A to Fact B, always using historical records and logical inference as my guide. The hardback special edition even includes an appendix that separates fact from fiction. And the war stories told by George Edwards? Those are drawn from his own words, just as he described them.

Given your success across fantasy, sci-fi and historical genres, how do you choose

J. D. Edwards, celebrated author of Indomitable and The Faerie Chronicles, crafting transformative tales of myth, history, and humanity.

which genre best suits a new story idea?

Because I have ADHD, my mind is constantly jumping between ideas and interests. Rather than fight that rhythm, I've learned to embrace it. I usually keep several manuscripts going at once and let instinct guide me toward whichever story has the strongest pull.

Right now, I'm halfway through writing The Defender of Faerie, a prequel to The Scions of Faerie. I've also started The Dark Realms of Faerie, which launches a new series, and I've revisited Dauntless, a historical fiction project I began in 2016. At any given time, it's not the genre that leads, but the heartbeat of the story. I write whichever one calls loudest that day.

Many of your protagonists undergo personal grief—how do you weave authentic emotional arcs while keeping plot momentum?

Everyone faces grief at some point; some more than others. It's not the pain itself that defines us, but how we respond to it. When tested by fire, do we become stronger, or do we shatter in the kiln of life?

That question is central to my novels. In 2004, after reading an early draft, George R. R. Martin told me: "Never create a character you're unwilling to kill." I've never forgotten his wise words. They've guided my storytelling ever since, reminding me that emotional honesty and plot momentum are not at odds. The loss has to matter. When it does, the reader feels it, and the story moves not just forward, but deeper.

Your background includes award-winning genealogical research—how does that rigorous detail enrich your world-building in speculative fiction?

My research is laborious, to say the least. While writing Indomitable, I tracked the phases of the moon to determine how much light Eliza Harris would have had as she made her way through the wilderness. I verified that every object, from a revolver to birthing techniques, matched the historical realities of the time.

It took longer to research the historical accuracy of Indomitable than it did to write the book itself. Whether I'm crafting historical or speculative fiction, the process is the same. I want every moment to feel lived-in and real, grounded in truth even when wrapped in fiction. That's how my stories come alive.

What one piece of advice would you give aspiring authors based on your journey through multiple genres and publishing formats?

Expect your first draft to be rubbish, but don't give up. Finishing the novel is the most important step. Everything after that is editing, refining, and reshaping. Sometimes, that means a complete rewrite.

I rewrote The Scions of Faerie four times before it was ready for publication. Indomitable only needed one full draft, but by then, I was a 20-year veteran. Even so, I rewrote the first few chapters several times, exploring different points of view until I found one that resonated. That version finally gave Eliza Harris a voice—the one that had been taken from her nearly 180 years ago.

You cannot have light without shadow."

J. D. Edwards

Literature, Human Rights, Climate Change, Thrillers, Advocacy, Speculative Fiction

RÉAL LAPLAINE

Explores High-Concept Thrillers and Global Crises

BY Z. ROBERTS | NEW YORK

Réal Laplaine's works invite readers to confront pressing global crises through the lens of speculative fiction. His novels weave intricate tapestries where personal narratives intersect with wider existential concerns, often questioning humanity's role within the greater cosmos. Drawing upon his background, from the quiet, reflective hours spent as a child beneath the stars, to his advocacy for human rights, Laplaine's writing serves as both a creative and moral compass.

With a profound commitment to sparking change, Laplaine's stories delve into the often harrowing realities of climate change, human trafficking, and social inequality. His books, such as The Other and See Me Not, are not mere thrillers but urgent calls for action, urging readers to consider the broader implications of the world they inhabit. His exploration of complex, real-world issues is deftly balanced with the tension and suspense of high-concept narratives, where every page is designed to keep readers not just entertained, but also aware.

The author's advocacy for literacy and fair representation in the literary world, through initiatives like International Writers Inspiring Change (IWIC), reflects his desire to give authors the respect they deserve while rekindling the love for books in an increasingly digital age. Laplaine's commitment to social justice, mirrored in his fiction, underscores the belief that literature has the power to shape minds, stir hearts, and ultimately, change the world.

In this interview, Laplaine reflects on the themes and motivations behind his work, offering an intimate insight into the thought process of a writer who believes that the pen, in its truest sense, is indeed mightier than the sword.

How did the inspiration for The Other —with its alien object off Ireland's coast and climate-change context—evolve from your interest in psychological thrillers?

As a kid, I used to climb on the roof of our house and sit there for hours staring at the sky and stars. It occurred to me then that clearly, in that ocean of stars there had to be more intelligent life like ours – and given the state of the world I found myself in at the time, I wasn't very impressed by our collective "intelligence". An avid fan of science-fiction, I found the depiction of "aliens" as most often aggressive and a threat to humanity, as a small-minded view of the Universe. ET, the film, of course, mollified that – thanks to Steven Spielberg's imagination. Given that global warming had been ramping up to a crisis point for years, and also inspired by a 16 year-old Swedish girl who lived just a few hours from me, Greta Thunberg, who made a stand and started a global tsunami on the subject, I decided to write THE OTHER and its sequel, L.I.N. to lend another perspective to the narrative – that maybe, off-worlders would come to Earth to help us save it before it is too late.

In truth, this idea or theme appears in several of my other books too, that is; WHEN GODS ROAR, TWILIGHT VISITOR, V.O.I.C.E. and EARTH ESCAPE.

In SEE ME NOT, you portray the horrors of trafficking through young hann'sha's eyes. How did blending fiction with real events shape your narrative approach?

In 2004, I was living and working in Los Angeles, when the Tsunami struck Southeast Asia. For a period, I headed up an initiative to send volunteers to India and other affected areas, to help. In Calcutta, our team came across homeless children, but one of them, a six-year-old girl, struck a chord in my heart, so deep and so unforgettable, because she was found living in a ditch with her one-or two-year-old brother, foraging for food and handouts. The team plucked them up, got them medical care, food, clothing and shelter, and sent me both the before and after photos of this girl. I will never forget the look of renewed hope in her eyes. Some years later, I sat down and researched

Réal Laplaine shares insights into his compelling thrillers that blend global crises, speculative fiction, and urgent social themes, aiming to inspire change through storytelling and his advocacy for literacy.

what happens to children like her and the shocking fact that homeless kids in India are often forced to be mules for drug runners or forced into sexual servitude. Young girls, virgins, are highly rated in the sex-trafficking industry there. SEE ME NOT was a "fictional" story about one girl, Hann'Sha, sold into sexual servitude at the age of eight (which happens often in very poor families there), who endures her slavery for four years before a young Canadian, visiting Calcutta, discovers and makes it his mission to free her – a task that sends him down some very perilous roads.

With Quantum Assault, part of the Keeno Crime Thriller series, how did you research the canadian trafficking ring to ensure authenticity?

The sex-trafficking pipeline and industry is a murky area to dig into, because of course, no one has accurate figures about just how many children and women are trafficked each year. However, when I released by book, SEE ME NOT, in 2012, I was introduced to a non-profit in Sweden, called RealStars, an initiative designed to export the Swedish model against sex trafficking. Essentially, Sweden is the first country in the world to criminalize buying sex – and working with the head of this initiative, she provided a lot of information obtained through her network with other similar organizations, moreover, her connections in Brussels, where she had been lobbying for laws that aligned to the Swedish model. I lectured at many of her events, whether in Stockholm at the International Anti-Trafficking events, at the International Women's Day in Gothenburg, at the International Swedish Book Fair and more. Quantum Assault, naturally followed in the footsteps of SEE ME NOT as a the 2nd book in my crime thriller series, using much of the information I learned in working with RealStars, moreover, research I did about the sex-trafficking pipeline through Canada's two main ports – Montreal and Vancouver.

Your background includes founding IWIC to promote literacy—how does your advocacy inform the themes in your recent works?

IWIC or International Writers Inspiring Change was never intended as a medium to promote myself as an author, but it is entirely based on two factors which inspired me to launch it in 2016. First, the fact that I was seeing a massive drop in reading. Younger kids, the Millennials, Gen X, etc., were observably not interested in reading books. Social media and the digital world had taken over. I saw this firsthand, because during this period, my wife and I had taken on several foster kids, giving them a home while they grew up, and clearly, there was absolutely no interest in reading. I recalled, growing up, that books were part of our culture. Getting on a bus, a subway, or going to the park, back in those early days, people had a book in their hands and were reading. Today, get on a bus, go anywhere, and all you see are mobile phones with people glued to them. I wanted to help put books back on the map.

Secondly, as an author, I was appalled to see the sheer number of book promotion sites and book sellers pitching to authors that they should offer their books for free or for 99cents. It was repulsive to me because I knew how much work authors put into their books – like me, the late nights, lots of sore eyes and coffee. I decided to launch IWIC to put prestige back into the subject and give authors a voice that also did not compromise their work and suggest that they should sell their books for the price of a cheesy hamburger. And by the way, I ran a campaign for a couple years, that a book is not equal in value to a hamburger. I think, I hope at least, given that even Amazon stopped offering authors the option to sell their books for 99 cents, that it had some impact.

You tackle complex global issues—climate,

62 || Reader's House

Réal Laplaine, Canadian-born author and advocate, shares his unique approach to blending fiction with urgent social issues.

trafficking, inequality—in high-concept thrillers. How do you balance message with suspense to keep readers engaged?

Yeah, this is THE trick – writing a story that captures the reader's imagination, thrills them, and also doesn't sound like I am standing on a soapbox. It's like riding a bike, or a motorcycle in my case, you just learn how to keep that balance, because if you don't, you lose the readers, and I learned early in my writing career, from comments I received at the time from readers, that balance is important. I believe that every author, generally speaking, has a message in their books – the skill is to dress it up in such a way that the whole package arrives with the reader.

The other combines speculative fiction and thriller elements—how do you maintain tension while exploring existential ideas?

My approach to writing my books is really simple. I get the idea, the general plot, but I NEVER sit down and map it out. I never want to know how my book ends. I write the story, page by page, as if I am in it, living it, feeling it, experiencing it. If it keeps me engaged. If I want to know what happens next, then I know I am on the right track. If I lose interest, or it becomes banal, I know I have derailed somewhere and I go back. In short, if my own writing thrills me to the end, then I know that it will do the same for others.

As a montreal-born author writing about global crises, how does your canadian identity influence your depiction of international issues?

I grew up in Canada during the 60's and 70's before moving to the States when I was twenty-one. Canada is not like its neighbor to the south. A very different dynamic runs through the blood of Canadians, at least it did then, but I believe it is still the case today. Canadians are very proud and independent. They do NOT identify themselves with Americans and resent it if anyone suggests so. Canada is two nations in one – that is French and English (British primarily) – and during the 70s, as more immigration opened up, The cultural diversity of Canada gives it a unique vibrance, making it feel more like Europe in its multicultural essence and I can say that now since I have lived in Europe for the past 15 years. Moreover, the things we saw as young men and women, the Vietnam War, political corruption (Nixon and Watergate), the loss of iconic and true leaders (JFK, Bobby Kennedy and Martin Luther King) was all happening across the border to the south of us. It repulsed us, it made us want to change the world to keep that away from our corner of the world. So, in many ways, growing up in Canada, despite some of the negative personal experiences, was quite liberating. Lastly, I created my own crime series called the Keeno Crime Thrillers, a character somewhat loosely based on myself and all the qualities that I think Canadians hold dear, so that Canada would have its own crime-fighter, which it lacked at the time.

What single piece of advice would you give to aspiring authors hoping to write high-concept thrillers with real-world significance?

I don't want to sound one-sided on this, but I think authors jumping into this pond should figure out what message they want to give the world through their books – and try to keep that thread in the weave of all their books, whether crime, romance, whatever. I believe that authors have an inherent duty to help inspire a better world – to plant seeds in the minds of readers. When I was 19 years old, trying to get a leg up on what I was going to do in life, a friend handed me the book *Jonathan Livingston Seagull* by Richard Bach. It's a simple story, but the message was so powerful, that it launched me into the life I led. That is the power that authors have – molding words, weaving worlds, and inspiring minds.

> *My goal in life was to change the world, to make a better world."*

Réal Laplaine

A Journey Through Character, Creativity And Inspiration

RUSSELL PIKE

Explores Moral Dilemmas And Epic Fantasy in Journey of Seven Circles

BY Z. ROBERTS | NEW YORK

Russell Pike's work is a testament to the enduring allure of epic fantasy and the power of storytelling to challenge, inspire, and transport. A writer whose own journey has been grounded in both passion and perseverance, Russell brings a unique voice to the genre, combining a love for rich, immersive worlds with an intellectual honesty that invites readers to grapple with the same moral complexities as his characters. His debut, *Journey of Seven Circles*, is every bit as profound as it is imaginative—a tale that begs to be savoured, questioned, and revisited.

With influences spanning titans of speculative fiction such as Robert Jordan, Anne McCaffrey, and David Farland, Russell doesn't merely follow in their footsteps; he charts his own course, crafting a blend of magic and World War I-era technology that feels refreshingly original yet profoundly authentic. His protagonist Kryn Darien is more than a hero—he's a mirror held up to the human experience, navigating a world that is as morally intricate as ours. And while Russell's meticulous world-building may avoid the encyclopaedic pitfalls of the genre, it is no less vivid, focusing keenly on the aspects that bring depth and resonance to the narrative.

Beyond his creativity, what shines through is Russell's absolute commitment to the craft. His structured approach, disciplined writing routine, and reverence for feedback—particularly the mentorship of the late David Farland—speak to a writer who has worked tirelessly to hone his skills. Yet his journey isn't simply one of deadlines and drafts. His love of nature, his sled-dog adventures, and his invincible optimism all find echoes in his stories, lending them a grounded humanity even amidst the fantastical.

It is an honour to present this conversation with Russell Pike, a rising luminary in the world of modern fantasy. In the interview that follows, we delve into the mind behind *Journey of Seven Circles*, exploring his inspirations, his process, and the wisdom he offers to aspiring writers. For regular readers of *Reader's House* and those discovering Russell for the first time, this promises to be a journey worth taking.

What inspired you to create the character of Kryn Darien and his journey in Journey of Seven Circles.

The idea behind Kryn Darien was to create a genuinely moral character, then mercilessly hurl a series of thorny dilemmas his way. At the beginning of Kryn's career, he's already developed a strong moral compass, however, his understanding of the world is somewhat simplistic. He isn't allowed to stay that way.

I believe most of us can feel echoes of this in our own lives. We form opinions early but are forced to reevaluate through experience. Hopefully, we grow deeper over time.

I wanted to highlight this growth in Kryn, but, I didn't want to spell out each lesson he learned. I don't even wish to force readers to

Russell Pike discusses his writing process, character development, and world-building in this insightful interview about his epic fantasy novel Journey of Seven Circles.

side with Kryn's decisions. Instead, I'd rather everyone decide for themselves the most important truth from each of Kryn's metaphorical circles.

How did your love of epic fantasy shape the world-building in your novels?

A good fantasy book can feel as much like exploration as reading. It's one of my favorite strengths of the genre. However, it can go too far. One of the most common complaints about fantasy is that some chapters feel like encyclopedia entries. I must admit it's a fair critique.

For that reason I kept the world-building in Journey of Seven Circles selective. Kryn goes to war, but we don't discuss the war's geopolitical causes. Kryn isn't a politician, so that isn't important to the story. All we need to know is why Kryn goes to war. The Church of the Seraphs receives more attention, but Kryn's principles represent such a large part of his character, the story demands the detail.

Lastly, I love to mix up concepts and ideas to freshen up the genre. In Journey of Seven Circles, we combine magic and World War I era technology to put a twist on Kryn's world.

Could you share more about your writing process – do you have a particular routine or approach?

I used to be night owl, but then I started working a job that began at three fifteen in the morning. It took a couple of years to beat my circadian rhythms into submission, but now my creative juices flow best in the morning.

As to my approach, I'm a hardcore outliner. I don't feel comfortable beginning page one unless I know exactly how each chapter is to be handled. I've found this has greatly improved my writing speed since I spend far less time backtracking to fix mistakes or add in new ideas.

How did your experience working with David Farland influence your writing career?

I've often described David as the world's gentlest drill sergeant. The first time he edited one of my manuscripts, he kindly told me what a fine job I'd done right before bleeding red ink all over the page. With the second manuscript, he told me how much I'd improved, then once again ripped my work to shreds.

It was a blow to my ego, but as I followed his advice, I couldn't deny my work was improving. The last manuscript I sent him was in 2021. I expected another red-inked evisceration, but this time he had nothing but good to say, telling me I was ready. I felt like a young knight who'd been handed a magic sword by a wizard and sent to slay a dragon. Dave died a few months after that last conversation, but his final vote of confidence helps keep my spirits up to this day.

Russell Pike's *Journey of Seven Circles* is an enthralling blend of epic fantasy and moral exploration. With masterful world-building and a compelling protagonist in Kryn Darien, the novel weaves themes of sacrifice and human resilience into a magic-fuelled adventure. A gripping debut, it's sure to captivate readers craving depth and originality.

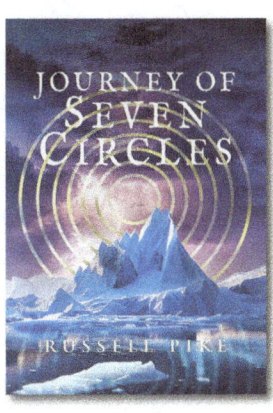

Russell Pike: The rising voice in epic fantasy, blending moral complexity with fantastical worlds in his acclaimed debut *Journey of Seven Circles.*

Which authors have had the most profound impact on your own writing style?

The first epic fantasy book I ever read was Eye of the World by Robert Jordan, and I was instantly sucked into the fantastic world and vast cast of characters. While this spurred my love of the genre, I've learned more techniques from David Farland than any other author.

Outside of writing, how do your hobbies, like camping and sled dog handling, influence your storytelling.

One of the lead dogs I worked with was named Tracer. He wasn't the fastest dog, but he was stalwart even by the high standards of Alaskan huskies. In fact, he'd often outperform faster dogs on bad trails, simply because he refused to be fazed by temperature, bad trail conditions, or heavy snow. His attitude holds a lesson for us all.

What advice would you give to aspiring writers who are just starting out in the fantasy genre?

Don't write your magnum opus first. I tried, and it didn't work. Instead, pick an idea you like but aren't in love with, then work it into a novel. Aim for about fifty thousand words. The end result will likely be terrible, but that's fine. Don't expect to paint a masterpiece the first time you pick up a paintbrush.

Once you have a manuscript, invite some critique from your peers, edit it a few times, then put it away. (My first practice novels are buried in the metaphorical desert. The location shall never be revealed.) Start over from the beginning with a new idea and repeat the process. You may be surprised how much more quickly your skills grow when you use this method.

A good fantasy book can feel as much like exploration as reading."

Russell Pike

Reader's House || 65

Exploring Love, Identity, and Self-Acceptance Through Character-Driven Stories and Humour

Daryl Banner discusses his bestselling Spruce Texas series, the emotional depth behind his characters, the balance of humour and heartbreak, and why writing romance is both a passion and a purpose.

DARYL BANNER

Shares How Music, Psychology, and Small-Town Stories Shape His Unforgettable Gay Romance Novels

USA Today Bestselling Author

"Bridger just can't hold back from criticizing Anthony's recklessness, and Anthony can't help but 'poke the bear' of Bridger's stoicism."

Editor's Desk | London

Daryl Banner brings a bold blend of heartfelt emotion, wit, and musicality to the pages of his beloved romance novels. A USA Today Bestselling author with a background in theatre and psychology, he infuses his stories with both narrative depth and dramatic flair. His Spruce Texas Romance series—beginning with Football Sundae—has blossomed into a fan-favourite collection exploring love, identity, and self-acceptance in a small-town setting. With dynamic characters who tug at readers' hearts and dialogue as rhythmic as a melody, Banner captures the complexity of human connection with both humour and vulnerability. Whether writing opposites-attract love stories or crafting sweeping, time-spanning sagas like When I See You Again, he invites readers to witness characters breaking free of their emotional armour to discover something real. In this exclusive interview, Banner reflects on his creative journey, the psychology behind his characters, and why writing romance has become more than a calling—it's a mission.

What first inspired you to write the Spruce Texas Romance series, and did you always envision it becoming a long-running series?

I wanted to reinvent my own experiences growing up gay in Texas, which is how I came about writing Football Sundae, the first book in the Spruce Texas series. It was intended as just a stand-alone romance, but after receiving so much love from readers, I realized there were many more stories to tell in Spruce. I just released the 9th book "Hot Mess Express" with a 10th in development and am still having so much fun writing them, which I suppose is a good sign!

"Hot Mess Express" features a strong contrast between Bridger and Anthony—how did you balance the tension and humour in their relationship?

Honestly? I didn't. I let them go way off balance whenever it pleased them. Bridger is uptight and controlling, recently discharged from the Army. Anthony is wild and unapologetic. At moments it felt like the scenes were writing themselves. Bridger just can't hold back from criticizing Anthony's recklessness, and Anthony can't help but "poke the bear" of Bridger's stoicism. I loved letting these guys "take the lead" in directing the plot, more or less, having faith they'll find their own balance once they open up to each other. And boy, do they ever.

How do you go about developing such dynamic chemistry between your characters, particularly in opposites-attract scenarios?

One of the most profound things I learned pursuing my degree in psychology was the myth of "opposites attract", which still to this day affects my writing. We build walls and defenses through our lives to protect ourselves from being hurt, and underneath, there's a vulnerable part that never changes, like our inner child. That's where alleged opposites find their common ground. I have so much fun playing with the idea of what people seem like versus who they really are inside. It's tively to Noah, noting he seems neurodivergent and seeing themselves in how he navigates the world. The love interest Cole is a "perfect" (pun intended) complement to Noah.

How do your skills as a composer influence your storytelling? Do you find similarities between writing music and writing fiction?

When I compose, I always keep a story in my head. I've been composing since I was a kid and was mostly inspired by video game music growing up, which might explain why I've always experienced music as a story. I never skip tracks when I listen to an album because I feel like it's the same as skipping chapters in a book.

What's your process like when starting a new book—do you plot thoroughly or let the characters lead the way?

Usually, my books start with a single idea: a character, situation, or concept. Then I think about it—a lot. It's important for the story to develop organically and not be contrived, which is something my time as a theatre/playwrighting major in college taught me. Outlining can be useful if your story has many moving parts (like my dystopian and fantasy series). But I still need to leave space for the characters to "play". My favorite thing is surprising myself: "Oh, they want to do this now? Okay, let's see what happens." Isn't that how life is sometimes?

"When I See You Again", an Amazon Celebrity Pick of 2021, touches on family dynamics and personal responsibility. How do you weave deeper emotional themes into a romantic plot?

"When I See You Again" is one of my favorite stories I've written, and that's due to its deeper themes and unique storytelling structure, with every chapter taking place 5 years later. I sat on the idea for many years, unsure how to tell the story of Caleb and Beau, and scrapped my first chapter probably four times before finally finding the "voice" of the book. I set out to showcase how love can grow in unlikely places over the course of an entire lifetime as well as how that love can change—from curiosities felt as children, to the turmoil of teenage crushes, to juggling the burdens of young adult life and beyond. The story continues beyond the happily-ever-after. My challenge as an author was writing complex, sometimes painful scenes while also preserving the humor, heart, and excitement of falling in love. Stories can amuse and arouse you with the same amount of intensity as they can devastate.

What advice would you give to aspiring authors hoping to build engaging, heartfelt romance series that resonate with readers?

As cliché as it sounds: stay true to yourself. From my own experience, I can say you won't remember the release of any specific book. You won't remember that one awful thing that one person said. Or the crick in your neck from hunching over the keyboard for hours. What you'll remember is the indescribable glory of

Hot Mess Express follows Bridger, a stoic Army vet seeking peace in Spruce, Texas, who clashes with Anthony, a chaotic party boy. Their fiery enemies-to-lovers journey unfolds with humour, heart, and heat, as tension turns to unexpected romance in this steamy, small-town M/M love story full of personality.

> Daryl Banner masterfully blends wit, warmth, and vulnerability, crafting emotionally rich romances that resonate deeply with readers around the world.

like a smirking promise of what's to come when these "seeming opposites" collide.

Your books often explore themes of identity and self-acceptance. How important is it for you to represent these journeys in small-town settings?

Readers regularly comment wishing Spruce, Texas actually existed, because they love "living there" in the pages and feel the town and my characters give them hope. I was brought to tears from an email I got recently where a gay man said that through my books, he "experienced the love life he always wanted" and felt he'd missed out on. It makes me feel like my being an author is less of a career and more of a mission.

Do you have a favourite character from the Spruce Texas or Texas Beach Town series, and if so, what makes them special to you?

I'm so afraid to pick a favorite and have all the rest glare at me. But I choose Noah from "Mr. Picture Perfect". He lives inside his head, which is me in a nutshell. Many readers reacted posi-

writing that unexpected dramatic scene. You'll remember the passion in your heart when a new brilliant idea occurred to you mid-chapter. You'll remember when you were brave enough to "go there" and choose the risky option for your story, challenging yourself. You'll remember the pain of realizing a character must die despite your efforts to save them. It's the "moments" that will mean the most to you as an artist. Stay true to yourself and to the stories you wish to tell, no matter how strange they seem or how far they stray from what others are reading right now. If you can forgive me for being an overdramatic poetic mess: That unwritten story living in your heart right now is your prisoner, and you are (literally) the only person on the entire planet who can free it. The key is to make solid choices, risk making mistakes along the way, and just write. It is absolutely your responsibility to free that story. You're the hero of your inspiration. Rescue it, care for it, and set it aflight.

Crafting Stories Of Horror, Satire, And Adventure

MIKE MILLER

Explores Versatility, Creativity And An Unmatched Dedication To Cross-Genre Storytelling

BY BEN ALAN | LONDON

Mike Miller is a veritable powerhouse of creative storytelling whose prolific works have captivated audiences across a stunning array of genres. A graduate of U.C. Berkeley and WGU, and living in L.A. with his children, Mike has carved out a remarkable career that defies categorisation and embraces versatility in its truest sense. Whether plunging readers into the frosty horror and adventure of *The Yeti*, delivering biting satire with *Promoted*, or crafting the ultimate action-packed spectacle in *Garrison Rex*, he demonstrates an unparalleled ability to shape compelling narratives imbued with wit, intensity, and imagination.

Perhaps one of Mike's most striking accomplishments is his extraordinary *3VIL* series, a trilogy that masterfully evolves characters and escalates terror across its pages while breaking free from predictable horror conventions. Beyond prose, his expertise extends to the realm of screen subtitling and translation, where he's contributed to some of the largest franchises in entertainment history, from *The Lord of the Rings* to *The Simpsons*. This rich professional background seeps into his writing, adding layers of precision and polish to his dialogue and pacing.

Mike's brilliance lies in his fearless embrace of storytelling that entertains and enlightens, blending "high/low brow" elements with sharp narrative instincts and deep thematic resonance. With influences as broad as Vonnegut and Kubrick shaping his approach, he is a writer who surprises, inspires, and pushes the boundaries of genre with every project. In this interview, we delve into the mind of this exceptional author, exploring the roots of his creativity, the craft behind his most beloved works, and his advice for aspiring writers eager to embark on their own cross-genre adventures. Prepare to step into the fascinating world of Mike Miller, a master craftsman of stories that challenge, thrill, and endure.

In *The Yeti*, you blend horror with adventure—how did your personal fascination with myths influence the portrayal of the *Yeti* as both terrifying predator and enigmatic creature?

There's something primal about the legends all humans share. I felt like the abominable snowman never got his proper due, so I wrote the book I wanted to read - historical adventure + horror - and hope that it reads like a forgotten Victorian classic. For the horror aspects, it's key to keep things mysterious - the fear of the unknown really drives the reader's mind to imagine the worst possible things. I made the Yeti to be both the unstoppable apex predator to give our intrepid heroes the hardest time, but also wanted to keep so many of its motives, origins and abilities largely secret throughout the text to heighten the experience.

Promoted carries sharp humour and social commentary—what inspired the satirical take on corporate culture, and how much reflects your own experiences?

Promoted comes very much from my

Mike Miller discusses his creative process, inspirations, and career highlights, unveiling the storytelling secrets behind The Yeti, Promoted, Garrison Rex and the 3VIL series in an insightful interview.

experience of working at dead-end jobs. If you're "lucky" enough to find the right kind of corporate hellscape, then you quickly discover that your performance doesn't matter, and that the inept lords of middle management control any would-be success. So this book's wish fulfillment is twofold - rising up the ranks while getting revenge on your unworthy superiors. I feel this is how the real world works figuratively, so why not put it down as a crazy - yet informative - book?

Garrison Rex features a strong lead—how did your background in screenwriting shape the pacing and character arcs in that novel?

I wanted to write the ultimate action film, and the best ones border on the ridiculous. I wouldn't say that John Wick and Batman are comedies, yet when they're rolling unstoppably through bad guys, the audience can't help but laugh at the awesome adrenaline. So indeed Garrison Rex is my nominee for the ultimate protagonist, a hero whose skills and powers are so supreme that they go over the boundary of realism, yet there is nothing truly sci-fi or fantastic here. And for the proper build and pace, he faces enemies of escalating strength before the biggest bang I could conjure.

Your *3VIL* series spans multiple volumes—how did you sustain thematic tension across the trilogy while evolving each character's journey?

3VIL is my horror anthology series, because frankly horror often devolves down to simpler tricks and gimmicks that generally are not sustained well across an entire novel. But for me, I always want to write something I've never experienced before, so each story has relatively fresh spins apart from the classic tropes. No basic "zombie" or "ghost" stories here. I suppose *3VIL*'s common DNA might include "psychological madness" and "eldritch unknown Lovecraftian" horror, yet some of my personal favorites in there are very grounded in reality.

You've written across genres—from horror to comedy—how do you decide which narrative tone best suits a particular story premise?

I definitely like melodramatic genres, and think that any one of my stories still has other elements in there to round out the experience. To me they all share the idea of surprise - from horror's jump scares, to a big comedic punchline, to romance's tricky emotions, or to a startling mystery twist. But ultimately I think every story should primarily commit itself to one genre, because trying to evenly mix the two usually ends up confusing the reader. Any strong plot will not let you pretend it is any other genre but what it was born to be.

Your work in subtitling major films and games seems diverse—how has that experience influenced your prose style or dialogue choices?

After thousands of hours of "Hollywood" media, you see how efficient dialog needs to

Kill Thy Neighbor by Mike Miller is a gripping blend of dark comedy and chilling suspense. With sharp writing and an intriguing premise, it hooks readers into a surreal nightmare filled with mystery and tension. The clever narrative twists and ominous themes keep you captivated until the very last page. A must-read!

be, from the smallest indie films to the biggest blockbusters. And even reality TV now has certain demands of pacing for modern audiences. I always enjoyed reads that are propulsive roller-coasters rather than ones that literarily simmer in tone, thought and emotion. No reason not to do both! So I'd hope that my writing always serves both masters - to both entertain AND enlighten. Nobody likes writers who write for themselves or are unsure of where to take a story. To that end I have works fully outlined so I know how to get in and out of every beat without wasting anyone's time.

Given your influences ranging from Kurt Vonnegut to Kubrick, could you highlight a moment in your recent works where one such influence is most evident?

I've always admired and emulated writers whose work is uncategorizable. These masters balance both an enjoyable experience that also educates along the way. And they'll do things so well that audiences can be taken aback at how layered and nuanced their works are. I've always fancied the expression "high/low brow" as the right blend of elements to infuse in a work. My works like The Yeti and Promoted proudly honor Vonnegut's tradition of whimsical illustration. Recently I've been on a Wes Anderson kick, where I've seen my more recent works "Die Alive" and "Swipe Rite" borrowing from his sharply-crafted exposition and settings to better set up the scenes and themes to come with plot and characters. While those two are upcoming horror stories for my next 3VIL entry, they still viscerally shock and thrill with some new and improved characterization and world-building.

Finally, what one piece of advice would you give aspiring authors trying to build a versatile, cross-genre writing career?

Absorb everything. While it's easy to stay in our lanes for our preferred forms of entertainment, it's crucial for all writers to expose themselves to works outside of their comfort zone to properly stretch and grow. Please read and watch stories that seem beyond your wheelhouse, where even the "bad" works can teach authors how to be better. The best narrative work in any genre still must serve the foundation of plot, theme, character and emotion. So even if you're working on a slasher story, the best version will still have deeper thoughts and feelings to round out the experience and connect with the audience on multiple levels.

I write mystery-thrillers and literary fiction for adult readers who seek insight, fascination, and delight in the adventures of their own lives."

Mike Miller

The Thrilling Conclusion to The Price Of Trilogy

MICHAEL C BLAND

Explores the High-Stakes Cost of Freedom in His Award-Winning Science Fiction Trilogy

BY Z. ROBERTS | NEW YORK

Michael C Bland is a master of speculative fiction, weaving gripping narratives that not only entertain but also provoke deep thought about the intersection of technology and personal freedom. His award-winning "The Price Of" trilogy, which began with *The Price of Safety* in 2020, has captivated readers with its chillingly plausible vision of a near-future world where surveillance dictates every aspect of life. The second instalment, The Price of Rebellion, built upon this foundation, earning widespread acclaim and multiple literary awards, including Best Science Fiction Novel of the Year by Indies Today. Now, with the highly anticipated release of The Price of Freedom, which came out on April 8th Bland is set to deliver a thrilling conclusion that promises to challenge our perceptions of autonomy, resistance, and the cost of true liberty.

Bland's ability to craft a technologically advanced yet hauntingly realistic world stems from his meticulous research and keen understanding of contemporary trends. His exploration of surveillance, AI, and biosecurity is not just fiction—it is an urgent reflection on our own evolving digital landscape. Through his protagonist, Dray Quintero, he has created a hero whose transformation from an obedient engineer to a battle-scarred revolutionary mirrors the internal struggle of those who dare to question authority. The stakes are high, the action relentless, and the emotional depth undeniable.

Beyond his novels, Bland is also a dedicated advocate for the writing community. As a founding member and secretary of BookPod, he has fostered a network where authors can support and uplift one another, demonstrating his commitment to both storytelling and the craft itself. His journey from debut novelist to acclaimed author is a testament to perseverance, skill, and an unyielding passion for speculative fiction.

In this exclusive interview, Michael Bland shares insights into his creative process, the inspiration behind his dystopian universe, and what readers can expect from The Price of Freedom. Prepare to be both enlightened and enthralled as we delve into the mind of a writer who dares to ask: How much of our freedom are we willing to sacrifice in the name of security?

What inspired you to explore themes of surveillance and personal freedom in your novel "The Price of Safety"?

I was inspired when I was riding the "L" one day when I lived in Chicago. Every single person in the train car that day was staring at their cell phone. I realized I could strip naked and no one would notice. Yet there were cameras in the car's ceiling. So, while no one was watching, someone could always be watching. We've grown accustomed to cameras watching us and our phones tracking us. Imagine what our lives will be like twenty-plus years from now? How extreme will that monitoring become? And if someone we love gets in trouble, how can we protect them if technology is always watching?

These questions inspired my series. Tech-

Michael Bland discusses the inspiration behind his The Price Of trilogy, the challenges of crafting realistic futuristic technology, his writing process, and what readers can expect from The Price of Freedom.

nology can improve our lives but can also be used against us. I wanted to highlight that risk. In The Price of Safety, Dray Quintero's 19-year-old daughter commits a crime. He covers it up to save her life, and he has to fight the very surveillance system he created to try to keep her and her sister safe. This leads them to a larger conspiracy that highlights what happens if we don't understand who is controlling the technology around us.

How did your research of and experience with technology influence the futuristic elements depicted in your "The Price Of" trilogy?

It directly influenced the world I created. I had to keep in mind the technology that's available to the characters in the books but also the technology being used against them. I had instances where I had to discard various ideas as they either didn't serve the story or match the technology. I also found inspiration in some of the devices the characters use or have to contend with.

Through it all, I tried to make the world as realistic and believable as possible. In fact, some of the technology I envisioned is already becoming real. The trilogy has a device called a DNA scanner. We shed dead skin cells and hair follicles. In the book, the DNA scanners suck those cells and hair follicles out of the air, scan the DNA, and identify you. A month after The Price of Rebellion was released, a company in California announced they'd created that very technology.

Can you share any challenges you faced while developing the character of Dray Quintero throughout the series?

I wanted to make him as believable as possible. I also wanted to portray his engineering side as accurately as I could. I am not an engineer but my grandfathers were. I asked a friend of mine, who is a successful engineer, to proof The Price of Safety to ensure that Dray's knowledge and actions were accurate from an engineering standpoint.

A key aspect of the story is Dray's growth. Over the course of the three novels, he transforms from a law-abiding family man into a battle-scarred hero who risks everything for the country's freedom.

With "The Price of Rebellion" receiving multiple awards, including Best Science Fiction Novel of the Year by Indies Today, how has this recognition impacted your writing journey?

Each award had been meaningful to me. They have provided validation of my writing ability and recognition of the hard work I put into each book. Although I was traditionally published, The Price of Safety was my debut novel. I'm sure I'm not the only author who wondered if their writing was good enough. The awards have erased that doubt. They also have encouraged readers to take a chance with this still-new author. The responses to the first two books have been fantastic, and I cannot wait for readers to experience how the trilogy ends.

The Price of Freedom delivers a gripping, fast-paced finale to Michael C. Bland's trilogy. Set in a chilling dystopia, the emotional struggles of Dray Quintero blend seamlessly with the suspense-filled escape plot. Bland masterfully explores themes of sacrifice and resilience, culminating in an unpredictable, satisfying conclusion. A thrilling and poignant read!

As a founding member and secretary of BookPod, how has your involvement in this community influenced your work?

The BookPod has been a great source of support. There are over 200 writers, editors, and other creatives in the group who not only support each other, we help each other. If someone needs advice or is looking for an entertainment lawyer (for example), they can turn to the BookPod. I've developed friendships through our online community. Writing is largely a solitary endeavor, so having that community really helps, especially when I'm on a fifth round of edits with my book and can barely see straight.

Could you provide insights into your editing process and how it has shaped your own writing style?

I not only edit the story after I've completed the rough draft, I get feedback and guidance from another author. We exchange chapters, so I will read a chapter of his work while he reads a chapter of mine. We provide line edits as well as overall edits of the story, suggesting where to improve, what to cut, etc. I study his notes and accept those that best serve the story. Then I edit the entire novel again. And again. Once I feel the story is ready, I submit it to my publisher. They perform their own edit, then after they're satisfied, they prepare the book for publication.

What can readers expect from the upcoming third installment of "The Price Of" trilogy, scheduled for release on April 8?

In The Price of Freedom, readers will experience the twists and turns Dray, Raven, and the others experience as they face incredible odds and heartbreaking choices that drive our heroes to the end of their difficult journey. Starting approximately one month after the end of The Price of Rebellion, Dray is imprisoned and alone. He finds help from an unlikely source, though it means putting his daughters in terrible danger. As the blurb reads:

He tried running. He tried fighting. This time, he must try something radically different. Something no one will see coming.

What advice would you offer to aspiring authors aiming to craft compelling science fiction narratives?

Writing is a craft. It can be fun and exciting to create stories, but to become a published author, you need to learn your craft. Take classes. Befriend other authors and learn from them. And put in the work. It's extremely rare for someone to be able to generate professional-level stories instinctively. Learning the mechanics of writing and structure and character development, honing your skills, and obtaining feedback are critical.

> *Each award has provided validation and erased doubts, encouraging readers to take a chance on this still-new author."*

Michael Bland

Available in
PRINT

Americas to Australia

Europe to Africa Reader's House is available over 190 countries and thousands of retaiers, platforms including Amazon, Barnes & Noble, Walmart, Waterstone's .....

ELECTRONIC

It is an electronic (flip book) format and interactive. Accessable from electronic devices like pc, smart phone, notepads..

ONLINE

All interviews, we conduct make them accessable online for free.

SOCIAL MEDIA

We are on Facebook, Instagram and X. Please follow us on social media
@readershousemag

contact us today for an interview opportunity at
editor@readershouse.co.uk

And so much more ...

Key Partnerships and Future Initiatives
Expanding the Boundaries of Authors and Books

Being featured in Reader's House means gaining visibility not just in print edition, but across the entire media spectrum in the US, UK, Europe and beyond

Key Media Partnerships:

- Associated Press (reaching 50%+ of global population)
- Benzinga (5M monthly visitors)
- Nexstar (68% U.S. TV household penetration)
- Major search engines: Google News, Google, Yahoo, Bing, Ask
- EIN Press Wire coverage
- NewYox Media magazines coverage (Mosaic Digest, Reader's House, CEO Vision, Beauty Prime...)

Broadcast & Digital Coverage:

- Major U.S. network affiliates
- 150+ million monthly radio website users
- 500+ UK media outlets
- Minimum 5 to 20 media placements per country (Albania to Zambia)
- Enhanced SEO positioning with quality backlinks from each media
- Optimized presence on e-commerce platforms)

Distribution Highlights:

- Available through major retailers including Amazon, Barnes & Noble, Walmart, Blackwells and Waterstones
- Available through local retailers Alaska to Wisconsin in the United States.
- Available in print LIFETIME
- Featured across 3000+ media platforms in the US, UK, Europe and beyond

contact us today for an interview opportunity at
editor@readershouse.co.uk